Fairytale Knits

Katharina Ritter

Fairytale Knits

SEARCH PRESS

Foreword

Hand-knitted clothing is back!

Gone are the days when only 'housewives' knitted. Nowadays, it is more likely to be young people who are attracted to knitting, both male and female. Even Hollywood stars have been known to pass the time on set with knitting needles and yarn. For some time now, knitting has enjoyed a completely new image as a welcome form of relaxation, as well as a productive and creative hobby.

Knitting is also quite easy. Plain and purl stitches alternate to produce, row by row, a unique piece of knitwear.

There is a lot of pleasure to be had along the way; not least that gorgeous feeling of soft yarn running through your fingers, and the result is a special item that cannot be bought anywhere. You will definitely receive a lot of compliments.

Give your creativity free rein. Experiment with different yarns, including luxury ones, and create interesting and unusual garments for you and your family.

You will find a wide range of new designs and fresh knitting ideas in this book. And you can rest assured that all the pattern instructions have been tried out by a professional knitter.

I wish you a lot of fun knitting your favourite items from this book and in trying out your own ideas too!

> Some of the designs in this book include some simple crochet, for which both UK and US crochet abbreviations are provided. In each case the UK term is given first, followed by the US term in brackets.

Contents

Snow Queen

Cardigan with wide collar

Snuggly, cosy and warm, this cardigan is practical yet sexy. Allow the super-wide collar to fall loosely over the shoulders or lift it up at the back to keep your neck warm.

Sizes

UK 8–10 and 12–14/US 6–8 and 10–12. The instructions for the different sizes are separated by a forward slash. If there is no slash, then the details are applicable to both sizes.

Materials and needles

- 600/650g (21/23oz) of worsted/aran yarn in natural white (the yarn used was 70% merino and 30% alpaca)
- 5.5mm (US 9, UK 5) circular knitting needle at least 60cm (23½in) long (the precise length is not important as you will be knitting in rows) or size needed to obtain the correct gauge
- Cable needle
- Stitch holder
- Blunt-ended needle

- 5 buttons, approximately 20mm (¾in) in diameter

Patterns

Ribbing: *knit 2, purl 2*; repeat from * to * as instructed. On the wrong side rows work all stitches as they appear to maintain the ribbing.

Cable pattern (multiple of 12 stitches plus 2): work following the chart. Only the odd (right-side) rows are shown on the chart. On the even (wrong-side) rows, work all stitches as they appear. Repeat the 12-row pattern.

Gauge

16 stitches and 24 rows worked in the cable pattern using 5.5mm (US 9, UK 5) knitting needles = 10 × 10cm (4 × 4in).

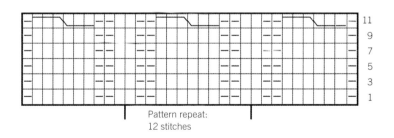

Pattern repeat: 12 stitches

☐ = knit 1

⊟ = purl 1

= place 3 stitches on to a cable needle in front of the work, knit 3, then knit the 3 stitches from the cable needle

Tip

The cable pattern pulls in part of the knit along the width, which is why the cast-off edge for these patterns can be slightly wavy. This can be prevented by knitting together the middle two stitches of every cable before casting off.

Instructions

Back

Cast on 82/86 stitches and work 10cm (4in) in ribbing as follows:
Row 1 (wrong-side row): work 1 selvedge stitch, knit 1, *purl 2, knit 2*; repeat from * to *, ending with knit 3, 1 selvedge stitch. Continue working in the established rib pattern until the piece measures 10cm (4in). On the next right-side row, begin working the cable pattern. The 1st right-side row begins with 1 selvedge stitch, purl 1, knit 6. Remember to read the chart from right to left (in the direction of the knitting).
Continue working in pattern, following the diagram.
Armhole: when the piece measures 53/55cm (21/21½in) from the cast-on edge, cast off on each side of alternate rows as follows: 4 stitches once, then 2 stitches twice and then 1 stitch twice [62/66 stitches].
When the piece measures 73/75cm (28¾ x 29½in) from the cast-on edge, put the middle 24 stitches on the stitch holder and finish both sides separately: cast off 2 stitches on the neckline edge

of the next row, work 1 row without shaping and then cast off 1 stitch at the neckline edge on the next row.
When the piece measures 75/77cm (29½/30¼in) from the cast-on edge, loosely cast off all the stitches.

Right Front (as worn)

Cast on 49/51 stitches and work 10cm (4in) in ribbing, incorporating the front welt in the knitting at the same time. The stitches in the 1st (wrong–side) row are therefore divided as follows: 1 selvedge stitch, knit 1, purl 6, *knit 2, purl 2,* repeat from * to *, ending with 1 selvedge stitch.

When the piece measures 10cm (4in), begin working in the cable pattern, retaining the stitches of the welt already established (do not work any cables on the welt). This results in the following distribution of stitches on right-side rows: 1 selvedge stitch, purl 1, knit 6, continue knitting in cable pattern.
Buttonholes: there are 5 buttonholes in the welt. On row 18 (right-side row), cast off the 2nd, 3rd and 4th stitches of the welt and cast them on again on the following row. Work the next 4 buttonholes in the same way, spacing them 22 rows apart.

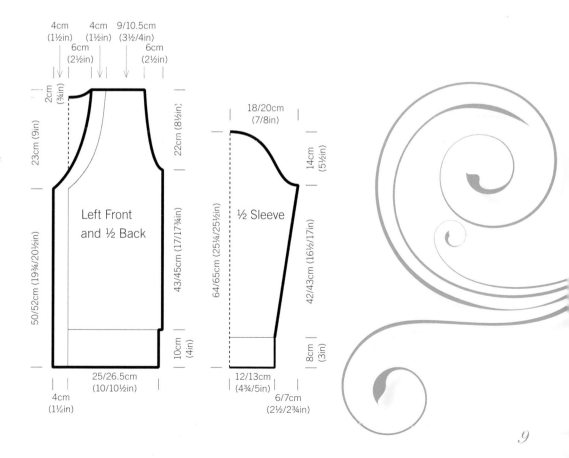

V-neck: when the piece measures 50/52cm (19¾/20½in) from the cast-on edge, on a right-side row, decrease 1 stitch by knitting 1 welt stitch to the following pattern stitch then continue in pattern. Maintaining the 5 remaining stitches of the welt in stocking stitch, decrease 1 stitch every 4 rows next to the welt 14 more times. At the same time, work the armhole shaping as follows.

Armholes: when the piece measures 53/55cm (21/21½in) from the cast-on edge work the armhole as described for the Back.

When the piece measures 75/77cm (29½/30¼in), loosely cast off all the stitches.

Left Front
Knit in a mirror image of the Right Front, but without buttonholes.

Sleeves (make 2)
Cast on 40/44 stitches and work 8cm (3in) in ribbing, starting the 1st (wrong-side) row with 1 selvedge stitch, purl 2, knit 2.

When the piece measures 8cm (3in), begin the cable pattern, working the 1st row (wrong-side row) as follows:

Size 8–10: 1 selvedge stitch, purl 2, knit 2, purl 2, knit 6 then continue knitting in cable pattern.

Size 12–14: 1 selvedge stitch, knit 2, purl 2, knit 2, purl 2, knit 6 then continue knitting in cable pattern.

On row 8/10 of the cable pattern, work the first cable. At the same time, increase

both sides by one stitch to create the slanted sleeve edges. Increase by 1 stitch another 9/10 times, every 8th row on each side.

When the piece measures 50/51cm (19½/20in), start decreasing for the sleeve head: cast off 4 stitches on each side then, on every other row, cast off first 3 stitches each side, then 2 stitches each side and finally 1 stitch each side. Knit 18 rows in the cable pattern.

Cast off on alternate rows as follows: 1 stitch on each side twice, then 2 stitches once and then 3 stitches twice.

Loosely cast off all stitches on the 2nd following row.

Work the second sleeve in the same way.

Assemble the pieces knitted so far, leaving the final stitches of the Back (at the neck) still on the stitch holder. Stretch out all the pieces, cover them with a damp cloth and leave them to dry. Join the seams and darn in the yarn ends. Attach the buttons to the welt of the Left Front in line with the buttonholes.

Tip
The collar is knitted on once the other pieces have been joined. So that the collar lies flat, you must cast on some additional stitches after a few centimetres. These will be hidden by the pattern.

Collar: Pick up the 24 stitches of the Back still on the stitch holder and knit in stocking stitch, increasing 1 stitch on

every row from the neckline on both sides. On row 7, loosely cast off all the stitches.

Starting 7cm (2¾in) above the top buttonhole on the Right Front welt and ending 7cm (2¾in) above the top button of the Left Front welt, pick up and knit 137 stitches for the collar. On the 1st (wrong-side) row, divide up the stitches according to the cable pattern: 1 selvedge stitch, purl 1, knit 2, purl 2, knit 6 (for the cable) then keep working following the cable pattern, ending with purl 2, knit 2, purl 1, 1 selvedge stitch. Work in cable pattern as established. Note that the right side of the collar lies to the inside, so that it is on the outside once the collar is turned down.

So that the collar sits nicely, increase by 1 purl in each purl-stitch rib on the 6th and 46th rows (right-side rows).

When the collar is 39cm (15½in) long, loosely cast off all the stitches and darn in the remaining yarn ends.

Stretch out the collar with the wrong side uppermost, cover with a damp cloth and leave to dry.

Fairytale Princess

Pretty party sweater

Knitwear can be so romantic. Pretty details like the satin ribbon and scalloped border on this sweater will make you feel like a princess.

Sizes

UK 10–12 and 14–16/US 8–10 and 12–14. The instructions for the different sizes are separated by a forward slash. If there is no slash, then the details are applicable to both sizes.

Materials and needles

- 450/475g (16/17oz) of sportweight/ 4-ply soft luxury yarn (the yarn used is 70% merino, 22% silk and 8% cashmere) in dark red
- 3mm (US 3, UK 11) knitting needles or size needed to obtain the correct gauge
- 3mm (US C-2, UK 11) crochet hook
- Blunt-ended needle
- 2m (2yd) of deep red satin ribbon, 10mm (⅜in) wide

Patterns

Ribbing: *knit 3, purl 3*, repeat from * to * on right side rows. Work all stitches on the wrong-side rows as they appear to maintain the ribbing.
Stocking stitch: knit right-side rows, purl wrong-side rows.

Gauge

27 stitches and 38 rows worked in stocking stitch using 3mm (US 3, UK 11) knitting needles = 10 × 10cm (4 × 4in).

Instructions

Back

Cast on 106/110 stitches and work in the ribbing pattern, decreasing 1 stitch on each side on rows 6, 12 and 18 [100/104 stitches].
When the piece measures 21.5/22.5cm (8½/9in) from the cast-on edge, start knitting in stocking stitch. On the 5th (right-side) row of stocking stitch, knit together every 9th and 10th stitch, then make a double yarn over; knit the yarn overs (to make one stitch) on the following wrong-side row to create the eyelets for the ribbon.

On the next row, increase by 22/28 stitches evenly distributed [122/132 stitches].
Armholes: when the piece measures 31.5/34.5cm (12½/13½in) from the cast-on edge, cast off 4 stitches at each end, then on alternate rows cast off 3 stitches once/2 stitches twice and then cast off 1 stitch 5 times/1 stitch 6 times, again casting off from each edge.
Neckline: when the piece measures 48/52cm (19/20½in), cast off the centre 52 stitches. Working on each side separately, cast off 2 stitches at the neck edge, work the next row without shaping then cast off another 2 stitches at the neck edge. When the piece measures 49.5/53.5cm (19½/21in), cast off the remaining stitches.

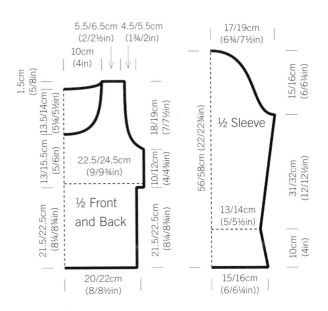

5.5/6.5cm (2/2½in) **4.5/5.5cm** (1¾/2in)

10cm (4in)

17/19cm (6¾/7½in)

1.5cm (5/8in)

13.5/14cm (5¼/5½in)

13/15.5cm (5/6in)

18/19cm (7/7½in)

15/16cm (6/6¼in)

10/12cm (4/4¾in)

½ Sleeve

22.5/24.5cm (9/9¾in)

56/58cm (22/22¾in)

½ Front and Back

31/32cm (12/12½in)

21.5/22.5cm (8¼/8¾in)

21.5/22.5cm (8¼/8¾in)

13/14cm (5/5½in)

20/22cm (8/8½in)

10cm (4in)

15/16cm (6/6¼in))

Front

Knit as for the Back, but for the neckline, cast off the centre 28 stitches when the piece measures 34.5/38cm (13½/15in). Now knit each side separately to the end, casting off at the neck edge of every other row 2 stitches twice and then 1 stitch 9 times. When the piece measures 49.5/53.5cm (19½/21in), cast off the remaining stitches.

Sleeves

Cast on 82/88 stitches and purl 1 row then continue knitting in stocking stitch (including a selvedge stitch on each side). When the piece measures 10cm (4in), knit together 2 stitches 10 times, evenly distributed. On the following right-side row work the selvedge stitch, knit 4, then knit 2 together, followed by a double yarn over (knit the yarn over on the following wrong-side row as before to make an eyelet),

then knit together each 7th and 8th stitch another 7 times, followed by a double yarn over.

For the slanted sleeve edge, increase 1 stitch 11/12 times every 8th row on both sides.

When the piece measures 41/42cm (16/16½in), cast off for the sleeve head on each side of every other row as follows: 4 stitches once, 3 stitches once, 2 stitches 2/3 times, 1 stitch 3 times. Next, on every 4th row cast off 1 stitch on each side 6/7 times. Now cast off on each side of every other row again: 1 stitch 4/5 times, 2 stitches twice, 4 stitches 3 times, 5 stitches once and then 6 stitches once. On the row after next, loosely cast off the remaining stitches.

Work the second sleeve in the same way.

Assembly

Stretch out all the pieces according to the pattern, cover with a damp cloth and leave to dry.

Darn in the yarn ends. Close the side, shoulder and sleeve seams and insert the sleeves.

Crochet around the neckline with 1 row of double crochet (US single crochet). On the next row, work the loops as follows: work 1 double crochet stitch (US single crochet), *crochet 4 trebles (US doubles) into the next but one stitch of the previous round, skip 1 stitch of the previous round, 1 double crochet stitch (US single crochet). * Repeat from * to * to the end of the row. Crochet around the edges of the sleeves in the same way. Thread a suitable length of satin ribbon through the eyelet holes around the body and sleeves and tie in a bow.

Frog Prince

Child's hooded jacket

Zip-fastened jackets with a hood are stylish and practical for children. Do not be afraid of inserting a zip fastener — you will easily learn how.

Sizes

2–3 years and 4–5 years.
The instructions for the different sizes are separated by a forward slash. If there is no slash, then the details are applicable to both sizes.

Materials and needles

- Cotton-blend worsted/aran knitting yarn: 50/100g (1¾/3½oz) in blue, 200/250g (7/9oz) in green
- 5mm (US 8, UK 6) knitting needles or size needed to obtain the correct gauge
- Blunt-ended needle
- Blue zip fastener (separable), 30/35cm (12/14in) long
- Sewing machine and blue thread to match the blue of the jacket

Patterns

Ribbing: *knit 2, purl 2,* repeat from * to * on right-side rows. Work all stitches on the wrong-side rows as they appear to maintain the ribbing.
Stocking stitch: knit right-side rows, purl wrong-side rows.

Gauge

16 stitches and 22 rows worked in stocking stitch with 5mm (US 8, UK 6) knitting needles = 10 × 10cm (4 × 4in).

Instructions

Back

Cast on 50/54 stitches in blue and work 4cm (1½in) in ribbing, including a selvedge stitch on each end.
Change to green yarn and continue knitting in stocking stitch.
Armholes: when the piece measures 18/22cm (7/8¾in) from the cast-on edge, cast off 2 stitches on each side, work 1 row without shaping then cast off 1 stitch on every other row 2/3 times.

Neckline: when the piece measures 30/34cm (12/13½in) from the cast-on edge, cast off the centre 12 stitches and finish both sides separately.
When the piece measures 32/36cm (12½/14in) from the cast-on edge, loosely cast off all the stitches.

Left Front (as worn)

Cast on 26/28 stitches in blue and work 4cm (1½in) in ribbing, including a selvedge stitch on each end.
Change to green yarn and continue knitting in stocking stitch.
Armhole: when the piece measures 18/22cm (7/8¾in) from the cast-on edge, work the cast offs on the right edge for the armhole as for the Back.
Neckline: when the piece measures 28/32cm (11/12½in), cast off 3 stitches from the left edge, work 1 row straight then cast off 1 stitch on every other row 3 times.
When the piece measures 32/36cm (12½/14in) loosely cast off all the stitches.

Right Front

Work in the mirror image of the Left Front.

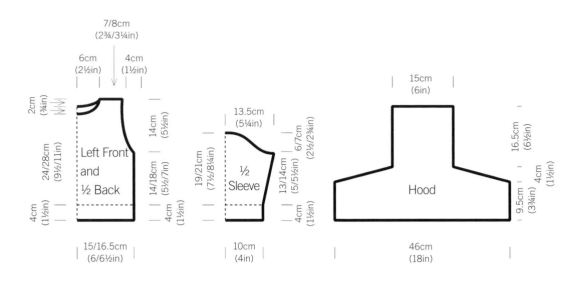

Measurements on diagrams:

7/8cm (2¾/3¼in)

6cm (2½in) 4cm (1½in)

2cm (¾in)

24/28cm (9½/11in)

Left Front and ½ Back

14cm (5½in)

14/18cm (5½/7in)

4cm (1½in)

4cm (1½in)

15/16.5cm (6/6½in)

13.5cm (5¼in)

19/21cm (7½/8¼in)

½ Sleeve

13/14cm (5/5½in)

6/7cm (2½/2¾in)

4cm (1½in)

10cm (4in)

15cm (6in)

Hood

16.5cm (6½in)

9.5cm (3¾in) 4cm (1½in)

46cm (18in)

Sleeves (make 2)

Cast on 34 stitches in blue and work 4cm (1½in) in ribbing.

Change to green yarn and continue knitting in stocking stitch.

For the slanted sleeve edge, increase 1 stitch on each side of every 6th row 6/7 times [46/48 stitches].

When the piece measures 17/18cm (6¾/7in) from the cast-on edge, cast off for the sleeve head on each side of every other row as follows: 4 stitches once, then 2 stitches once, 1 stitch 5/6 times, 2 stitches once and then 3 stitches once. On the row after next, loosely cast off the remaining 14 stitches.

Work the second sleeve in the same way.

Hood

Cast on 74 stitches in green and knit 9.5cm (3¾in) in stocking stitch. Then, at the start of each row cast off 5 stitches 10 times. On the remaining 24 stitches, knit another 16.5cm (6½in) in stocking stitch. Loosely cast off all the stitches.

Assembly

Stretch out all the pieces, dampen them and leave to dry.

Close up the shoulder and side seams. Close up the side seams of the hood (see the diagram). Sew the hood to the neck.

Pick up 55 stitches from the selvedge stitches of each Front piece using blue yarn and work 2 rows in stocking stitch. On the 3rd row, cast off all the stitches. From the same edge, cast on another 55 stitches and knit a second trim directly behind the first, as described above. (This will ensure that the zip fastener does not pucker after it is sewn in). Tack the zip fastener between both trims on each Front piece and sew in place using a sewing machine.

Pick up 74 stitches from the outside edge of the hood using blue yarn and work 5cm (2in) in stocking stitch. Loosely cast off all stitches. Turn this edge to the inside and sew in place to give a channel for the drawstring. Darn in all the yarn ends.

Cut a 120cm (47in) length of each yarn and twist the two together into a drawstring. Pull the drawstring through the channel at the front edge of the hood and knot the ends of the drawstrings to preven unravelling.

Tip

The jacket in the photographs has a contrast band on the sleeve just above the elbow. This can be added in Swiss darning (duplicate stitch) after the jacket is assembled or you can simply change to blue 14cm (5½in) above the cast-on edge of each sleeve, work 1 row in blue, 1 row in green, 1 further row in blue and then finish the sleeve in green as instructed.

Little Mermaid

Off-the-shoulder sweater

This off-the-shoulder sweater is very alluring, especially when knitted in a soft, fluffy yarn. Worked in an attractive uneven rib, it is really easy to knit.

Sizes

UK 10–12, 14 and 16–18/US 8–10, 12 and 14–16.

The instructions for the different sizes are separated by a forward slash. If there is no slash, then the details are applicable to all three sizes.

Materials and needles

- 200g (7oz) of mohair yarn in petrol blue
- 5mm (US 8, UK 6) knitting needles or size needed to obtain the correct gauge
- 5mm (US 8, UK 6) and 5.5mm (US 9, UK 5) circular knitting needles, 80cm (32in) long or size needed to obtain the correct gauge
- Blunt-ended needle

Patterns

Uneven ribbing: *purl 2, knit 4,* repeat from * to * on right-side rows. Work all stitches on wrong-side rows as they appear to maintain the ribbing. When working in rounds, work as right-side rows only.

Even ribbing: * knit 2, purl 2,* repeat from * to *. Working in rounds, knit each round the same.

Gauge

18 stitches and 26 rows in uneven ribbing using 5mm (US 8, UK 6) knitting needles = 10 × 10cm (4 × 4in) when slightly stretched.

Instructions

Back

Using the 5mm (US 8, UK 6) knitting needles, cast on 76/80/84 stitches and knit in uneven rib. On the 1st row (wrong-side row), divide the stitches up as follows: 1 selvedge stitch, *knit 2, purl 4,* continue knitting in uneven rib by repeating from * to * until the last 3 stitches, ending with knit 2, 1 selvedge stitch.

Armholes: when the piece measures 42/42/44cm (16½/16½/17½in), start decreasing for the armhole by casting off as follows on each side of alternate rows: 4 stitches once (row 1), then 2 stitches twice (rows 3 and 5) and then 1 stitch twice (rows 7 and 9).

Neckline: when the piece measures 59/60/63cm (23¼/23½/25in) from the cast-on edge, cast off the centre 30 stitches and finish both sides separately. Knit another 2cm (¾in) on each side in uneven rib and then loosely cast off the remaining 13/15/17 stitches at each shoulder.

Front

Work as for the Back until the piece measures 55/56/59cm (21¾/22/23¼in) from the cast-on edge.
Neckline: cast off the centre 20 stitches and finish both sides separately. On the side of the neckline, on every other row, cast off 2 stitches once (row 1) then 1 stitch 3 times (rows 3, 5 and 7).

Sleeves (make 2)

Using 5mm (US 8, UK 6) knitting needles, cast on 58/64/68 stitches and knit in uneven rib (1st row = wrong-side row).
Sleeve head: when the piece measures 50/51/52cm (19¾/20/20½in) from the cast-on edge, start the sleeve head by loosely casting off as follows on each side of alternate rows: 3 stitches once, then 2 stitches once and then 1 stitch 8/9/10 times.

When the piece measures 69/71/73cm (27/28/28¾in) from the cast-on edge, loosely cast off the remaining stitches. Work the second sleeve in the same way.

Assembly

Darn in all the yarn ends. Carefully stretch out all the pieces, cover them with a damp cloth and leave to dry.
Close the shoulder, side and sleeve seams and insert the sleeves.
Collar: Using the 5mm (US 8, UK 6) circular knitting needle, pick up 120 stitches from the inside of the neckline and knit in even rib (the right side of the piece is inside).
When the collar is 4cm (1½in) long, increase 1 stitch by picking up the bar between each pair of knit stitches [180 stitches] and start knitting in uneven rib. As the collar will be turned down to the outside later, the right side of the collar is towards the inside. When you turn the sweater inside out, the right side will be in front of you when you are knitting in rounds.
When the collar is 10cm (4in) long, change to the 5.5mm (US 9, UK 5) needle and continue knitting in uneven rib.
When the collar is 23cm (9in) long, loosely cast off all the stitches.
Slightly stretch the collar (wrong side uppermost), cover with a damp cloth and leave to dry.

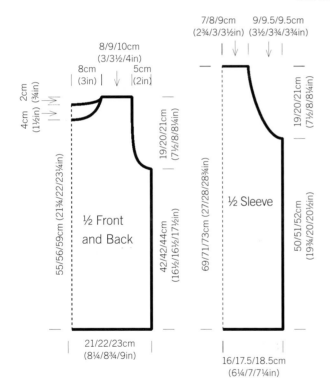

Snow White

Knitted stockings

Who still thinks that hand-knitted stockings are old-fashioned? These are very sexy! The attractive lacy design does, however, require some concentration.

Sizes

UK shoe size 3.5–9/US shoe size 5.5–11. (See table for details of individual sizes.)

Materials and needles

- 250g (9oz) of sock yarn in natural white
- Waste yarn in a contrasting colour or type e.g. smooth cotton yarn
- Set of 2.5mm (US 1, UK 13) double-pointed needles or size needed to obtain the correct gauge
- Blunt-ended needle
- 1.8m (2yd) of satin ribbon, 1cm (⅜in) wide
- Stitch marker

Patterns

Ribbing: *knit 1, purl 1*, repeat from * to *. Work each round the same.

Lace pattern: refer to the chart (number of stitches divisible by 8). Knit in rounds following the chart, repeating the 14-row pattern.

Gauge

26 stitches and 43 rows knitted in the lace pattern using 2.5mm (US 1, UK 13) knitting needles = 10 × 10cm (4 × 4in) when slightly stretched.

Tip

These stockings are easy to knit using short stocking needles made from bamboo, which can also be used for all other ankle and knee-high socks. They are only 15cm (6in) long.

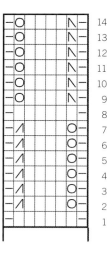

☐ = knit 1
⊟ = purl 1
Ⓞ = yarn over
◺ = knit 2 together
Ⓝ = slip 1, knit 1 then pass slipped stitch over

Stockings table

Shoe size/height	3.5–4.5 (US 5.5–6.5) 160cm (5ft 3in)	5–6 (US 7–8) 165cm (5ft 5in)	6.5–7.5 (US 8.5–9.5) 170cm (5ft 7in)	8–9 (US 10–11) 176cm (5ft 9in)
Cast on / stitches per needle	88/22	92/23	100/25	110/28
Decrease for calf (1st and 4th needles only)				
1st decrease after	26cm (10¼in)	27.5cm (10¾in)	29cm (11½in)	30cm (12in)
Every 8th round	4 times	4 times	5 times	6 times
Every 6th round	6 times	6 times	6 times	8 times
Every 4th round	4 times	6 times	7 times	9 times
Remaining stitches per needle	15	15	16	16
Leg height	34cm (13½in)	36cm (14¼in)	38cm (15in)	40cm (15¾in)
Heel				
Number of stitches for width of heel	30	30	32	32
Number of rows for height of heel	28	28	30	30
Number of stitches for cap	10/10/10	10/10/10	10/12/10	10/12/10
Cast on stitches on both sides	15	15	16	16
Foot				
Length of foot to start of toe	18.5cm (7¼in)	20cm (8in)	21cm (8¼in)	22cm (8¾in)
Toe (decrease)				
1st decrease on the 4th round	1 time	1 time	1 time	1 time
Every 3rd round	2 times	2 times	2 times	2 times
Every other round	3 times	3 times	3 times	3 times
Every round	6 times	6 times	7 times	7 times
Total foot length	23.5cm (9¼in)	25cm (10in)	26.5cm (10½in)	27.5cm (11in)

Instructions

Cuff

Provisional cast-on: cast on the number of stitches for each size according to the stocking table (see below) in a chain stitch using waste yarn, then continue knitting in ribbing using the main yarn. Mark the start/end of the rounds with a stitch marker.

Leg

When the cuff measures 3cm (1¼in) begin knitting in the lace pattern, following the chart (the eyelet section for the ribbon is worked later). If necessary, adapt the first and last part of the pattern. Decrease for the calf in the centre back (between the 4th and 1st needles), as indicated in the table. Adjust the design at the decrease.

Once the leg has reached the height stated in the table, start with the heel.

Heel

Knit 28 or 30 rows on the stitches of the 1st and 4th needles (see table). Then divide the stitches into 3 (see table) and knit the cap of the heel as follows: on the next right-side row, knit until the last stitch of the 2nd group, *slip the last stitch as if to knit and also slip the following stitch (1st stitch of the 3rd group). Turn the piece. Purl together both the slipped stitches, then knit all the stitches of the middle group as far as the last purl stitch. Slip this stitch as if to knit, along with the next stitch (1st stitch of the outer group) and turn the piece. Knit together both the slipped stitches. Knit the subsequent stitches of the middle group as far as the last knit stitch*. Repeat from * to * until all the stitches of both outer groups have been worked.

Foot

Keep knitting over all the stitches in rounds. Divide the heel cap stitches over 2 needles (1st and 4th needles). With the 1st needle, increase 1 stitch from each selvedge stitch of the left edge of the heel, between the 1st and 2nd needles, cast on 1 and knit through the back loop. Knit the stitches of the 2nd and 3rd needles. Between the 3rd and 4th needles, cast on 1 and knit through the back loop. From each selvedge stitch of the right edge of the heel, increase 1 stitch. Knit the remaining stitches of the 4th needle (= cap stitch).

There are now more stitches on the 1st and 4th needles than on the 2nd and 3rd needles. These stitches are cast off again for the gusset as follows: for the 1st needle, knit together the second- and third-last knit stitches; for the 4th needle, knit the 1st knit stitch, slip the 2nd knit stitch, knit the 3rd knit stitch and pass the slip stitch over. Repeat these decreases in each 3rd round, until the original number of stitches is reached again on all 4 needles.

Knit the foot in stocking stitch to the length shown in the table.

Toe

For the toe, decrease the work as shown in the table as follows: knit the stitches of the 1st and 3rd needles as far as the last 3 stitches, knit 2 together, knit the last knit stitch. For the 2nd and 4th needles, knit the 1st knit stitch, slip the following knit stitch, knit 1 knit stitch and pass the slip stitch over. Repeat these decreases at the intervals stated (see the table), until there are only 8 stitches left. Pull these stitches together tightly with a double yarn and finish the ends.

Assembly

Remove the waste yarn used for the cast on and thread the stitches on to the 4 needles again. Now work in the ribbing pattern. After 2cm (¾in) work an eyelet row as follows: knit together every 9th and 10th stitch and then work a double yarn over. (This yarn over knitted on the next row to make 1 stitch and therefore maintain the full number of stitches.) After another 2cm (¾in), very loosely cast off the stitches. Darn in the yarn ends. Thread half the satin ribbon through the eyelets, tieing the ends in a neat bow.

Work the second stocking in the same way.

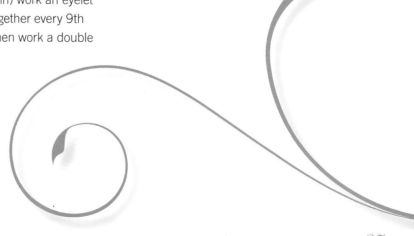

Sleeping Beauty

Fingerless gloves

The deceptively simple lacy pattern used for the stockings is repeated on these stylish fingerless gloves. As they do not require much yarn, take the opportunity to use a luxury fibre.

Sizes
One size: 27cm (10½in) long.

Materials and needles
- 75g (2½oz) of 4-ply/fingering yarn (the yarn used here is 70% merino, 22% silk and 8% cashmere) in natural white
- Set of 3mm (US 3, UK 11) double-pointed knitting needles or size needed to obtain the correct gauge
- Blunt-ended needle
- Stitch markers
- Stitch holder

Patterns
Lace pattern: refer to the chart (number of stitches divisible by 8). Knit in rounds following the chart, repeating the 14-row pattern.

Gauge
28 stitches and 36 rows worked in the lace pattern using 3mm (US 3, UK 11) knitting needles = 10 × 10cm (4 × 4in).

Instructions
Cast on 64 stitches and close up into a round, distributing 16 stitches on each of the 4 needles. Mark the start/end of the rounds with a stitch marker.
Knit 1 round of purl stitches.
Begin knitting the lace pattern, starting with round 7 of the chart. There are 8 pattern repeats. On your second round (round 8 of the chart) decrease 1 stitch in the first 8-stitch pattern only, working the next 7 pattern repeats following the chart. When you reach round 8 of the chart again, decrease 1 stitch on the second pattern repeat only. The next

−	O			N	−	14
−	O			N	−	13
−	O			N	−	12
−	O			N	−	11
−	O			N	−	10
−	O			N	−	9
−					−	8
−	⋏		O		−	7
−	⋏		O		−	6
−	⋏		O		−	5
−	⋏		O		−	4
−	⋏		O		−	3
−	⋏		O		−	2
−					−	1

☐ − knit 1
− = purl 1
O = 1 yarn over
⋏ = knit 2 together
N = slip 1, knit 1 and pass slipped stitch over

by picking up the yarn between two stitches and knitting it through the back loop after the 1st marker and before the 2nd marker. Repeat these increases 4 times in each 3rd round then 3 times on every other round and incorporate into the lace pattern. After a further round, put the stitches of the thumb gusset (17 stitches) on to the stitch holder. Now continue working on the remaining stitches of the hand, casting on 3 stitches over the stitches on the holder. Work 5 rounds in the lace pattern then knit 1 round of purl stitches, 2 rounds of knit stitches and 1 round of purl stitches. Loosely cast off all the stitches.

Thumb

Move the stitches from the holder on to a needle and cast on 3 stitches from the thumb bridge. Distribute these stitches evenly over 3 needles and knit 4 rounds in stocking stitch. Loosely cast off all the stitches. Make the second fingerless glove the same.

time, decrease 1 stitch on the third repeat and so on until you have worked decreases on the first 6 patterns [58 stitches].

Thumb gusset

Using the stitch markers, mark the 2nd and 4th stitches on the 3rd needle. The thumb gusset is knitted in between as follows: on the following rounds, make 1

Assembly

Darn in the yarn ends. If desired, the edges can be decorated by sewing on beads.

Elves and the Shoemaker

Baby bootees

Babies are always on the move, which means that shoes and socks are often lost. The satin ribbon ties on these bootees will help prevent that from happening.

Sizes
Suitable for babies up to 5 months.

Materials and needles
- 50g (1¾oz) of sock yarn in your chosen colour
- Set of 2.5mm (US 1, UK 13) double-pointed needles or size needed to obtain the correct gauge
- Blunt-ended needle
- Stitch marker
- 60cm (24in) of satin ribbon to match the yarn, 10mm (⅜in) wide

Patterns
Stocking stitch: knit right-side rows, purl wrong-side rows. When working in rounds, knit every round.
Reverse stocking stitch: working in rounds, purl every round.
Garter stitch: knit every row (when working in rounds, knit 1 row and purl the next).

Gauge
30 stitches and 42 rows worked in stocking stitch using 2.5mm (US 1, UK 13) knitting needles = 10 × 10cm (4 × 4in).

Instructions
Cast on 48 stitches and close up into a round, distributing 12 stitches on each of the 4 needles. Mark the start/end of the rounds with a stitch marker.
Rounds 1–4: knit in reverse stocking stitch.
Rounds 5–8: knit in stocking stitch.
Repeat rounds 1–8 twice more.

Round 25 (eyelet round): *knit 6, knit 2 together, yarn over,* repeat from * to * to the end of the round.
Round 26–29: knit in stocking stitch, working each yarn over of round 25 as a normal stitch.

Tongue
Leave the stitches of the 2nd, 3rd and 4th needles and knit 20 rows of stocking stitch over the stitches of the 1st needle only.

Foot
Cast on 11 stitches from the side of the tongue, knit the stitches of the 2nd, 3rd and 4th needles, then cast on 11 stitches from the other side of the tongue [70 stitches].
Continue knitting in rounds over all the stitches divided as follows:
1st needle: the 12 stitches of the tongue.
2nd needle: 11 stitches from the side of the tongue plus the 12 stitches already on the 2nd needle.

3rd needle: the 12 stitches of the edge of the heel.

4th needle: the 12 stitches already on the 4th needle plus 11 stitches from the side edge of the tongue.

* Purl 4 rounds, knit 4 rounds,* repeat from * to * once more and complete the foot with 4 purl rounds.

Sole

Starting from the toes, knit garter stitch in rows on the stitches of the 1st needle, but at the beginning of each new row knit together the first stitch with the nearest stitch from the adjacent (2nd or 4th) needle. Continue in this way until all the stitches of the 2nd and 4th needles have been incorporated.

Carefully turn the work wrong side out, without pulling the needles out of the stitches, before continuing. Now knit together 1 stitch from the 1st needle with 1 stitch from the 3rd needle. Loosely cast off the 12 remaining stitches.

Make the second boot in the same way.

Assembly

Darn in the yarn ends. Cut the satin ribbon in half. Thread a length of ribbon through the eyelets on each boot, starting and finishing at the centre front. Tie the ribbon ends in a bow and trim as required.

Tip

Little items such as these can easily be made using short bamboo double-pointed knitting needles.

Goldilocks

Lacy bolero

This is a very simple lacy pattern that is easy to learn and quick to work, making it an excellent project for anyone new to lace knitting.

Sizes

UK 10–12 and 14–16/US 8–10 and 12–14. The details for the different sizes are separated by a forward slash. If there is no slash, then the details are applicable to both sizes.

Materials and needles

- 350g (12½oz) of 4-ply/fingering linen-blend yarn in black
- 3.5mm (US 4, UK10) knitting needles or size needed to obtain the correct gauge
- Blunt-ended needle
- 1m (1yd) of black satin ribbon, 10mm (⅜in) wide

Patterns

Lace pattern: knit in rows following the chart.
Only the 1st row (right-side row) is marked. On the 2nd row and all subsequent wrong-side rows, purl all stitches and work yarn overs purlwise. Stocking stitch: knit right-side rows, purl wrong-side rows.

Pattern repeat:
10 stitches

☐ = knit 1
Ⓞ = purl 1
Λ =slip 2 together, knit 1 and pass the slip stitches over

Gauge

22 stitches and 28 rows worked in lace pattern using 3.5mm (US 4, UK10) knitting needles = 10 × 10cm (4 × 4in).

Instructions

Back

Cast on 95/105 stitches and purl 1 row. Begin knitting in the lace pattern following the chart and working 1 selvedge stitch on each end. (For size 14–16, at the start and end of the row, next to each selvedge stitch, knit 1; otherwise work following the lace pattern.)
When the piece measures 10cm (4in) from the cast-on edge, increase by 1 stitch on each edge. When the piece measures 15cm (6in), increase again by 1 stitch on each edge. (Now start every right-side row with 1 selvedge stitch, knit 3, 1 yarn-over etc.)
Armholes: when the piece measures 20cm (8in) from the cast-on edge, start decreasing for the armhole. Cast off the following on each edge on every other row: 5 stitches once, then 3 stitches twice and then 2 stitches twice, maintaining the lace pattern as set. (Every yarn over should be matched by a corresponding stitch decrease; if there is no yarn over due to the decreasing at the side, instead of 3 stitches, knit together just 2 stitches.)

When the piece measures 42/43cm (16½/17in) from the cast-on edge, loosely cast off all the stitches knitwise.

Right Front (as worn):

Cast on 53/55 stitches and purl 1 row, then begin knitting in the lace pattern following the chart. (For size 14–16, at the start and end of the row, next to each selvedge stitch, knit 1; otherwise work following the lace pattern.)

When the piece measures 10cm (4in) from the cast-on edge, increase by 1 stitch on the left edge. When the piece measures 15cm (6in), increase again by 1 stitch on the left edge.

Armhole: when the piece measures 20cm (8in) from the cast-on edge, decrease for the armhole on the left edge, as described for the Back.

Neckline: when the piece measures 32/33cm (12½/13in), start decreasing for the neckline by casting off the following on the right edge on every other row: 6 stitches once, then 4 stitches twice and then 2 stitches 3 times. When the piece measures 42/43cm (16½/17in) from the cast-on edge loosely cast off all the stitches.

Left Front

Work in the mirror image to the Right Front piece.

Sleeves (make 2)

Cast on 73/75 stitches and purl 1 row then begin knitting in the pattern. When the piece measures 12cm (4¾in) from the cast-on edge, increase by 1 stitch on each side, then increase 1 stitch every 10th row on each side 8/10 times. When the piece measures 44/45cm (17¼/17¾in), cast off the following on each edge on every other row: 5 stitches once, then 4 stitches once, then 3 stitches once and then 1 stitch 9/11 times. Work 6 rows in pattern without decreasing then cast off the following on each edge on every other row: 1 stitch 3 times, then 2 stitches twice, then 3 stitches once and then 4 stitches once. On the 2nd following row, when the piece measures 56/59cm (22/23in), loosely cast off all the stitches. Work the second sleeve in the same way.

Assembly

Stretch out all the pieces according to the pattern, cover with a damp cloth and leave to dry. Darn in the yarn ends. Close the side, shoulder and sleeve seams and insert the sleeves.

Neckline trim with filigree edging: cast on 96 stitches from the neckline on the right side of the work and knit 2 rows in stocking stitch.

Row 3 (right-side row of eyelets): work 1 selvedge stitch, knit 3, *yarn over, knit 2 together, knit 6,* repeat from * to * 10 times, ending with 1 yarn over, knit 2, work 1 selvedge stitch.

Knit 3 rows in stocking stitch.

Row 7 (filigree edging): work 1 selvedge stitch, *knit 2 together, yarn over,* repeat from * to *, ending with knit 2, work 1 selvedge stitch.

Knit 5 rows in stocking stitch.

Next row, loosely cast off all the stitches. Fold the neckline trim to the inside at the edge of the filigree edging and stitch in place. Thread the satin ribbon through the eyelets in the trim.

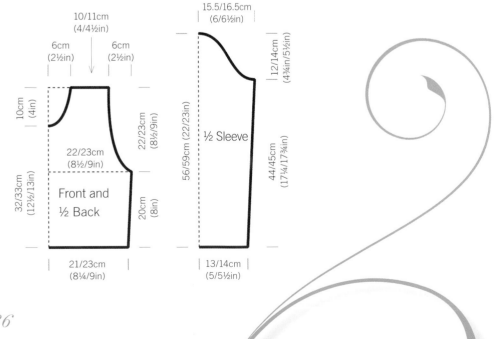

Little Red Riding Hood

Hat

This comfortable hat is reminiscent of a previous, more romantic era. Make several to match different outfits.

Sizes

Fits a 54–57cm (21¼–22½in) head circumference.

Materials and needles

- 100g (3½oz) wool-blend colour-graduated aran or chunky yarn in red
- 5mm (US 8, UK 6) double-pointed needles
- 6mm (US 10, UK 4) double-pointed needles or size needed to obtain the correct gauge
- 6mm (US 10, UK 4) circular knitting needles 60cm (24in) long, or size needed to obtain gauge
- Blunt-ended needle
- Stitch marker

Tip

For a strong transition from one ball of yarn to the next, knit 6 to 8 stitches with both yarns together.

Patterns

Stocking stitch: working in rounds, knit every round.
Ribbing: knit 1, purl 1 around. Work every round in the same way.

Gauge

17 stitches and 21 rows worked in stocking stitch using 6mm (US 10, UK 4) knitting needles = 10 × 10cm (4 × 4in).

Instructions

Using 5mm (US 8, UK 6) double-pointed needles, cast on 80 stitches and close up into a round, distributing 20 stitches on each of the 4 needles. Be careful not to twist the stitches when you begin the first round. Mark the beginning/end of rounds with a stitch marker. Knit 5cm (2in) in ribbing.

On the final round of ribbing, increase the stitches on the 1st and 4th needles by picking up the bar between the 1st and 2nd stitches, then *knit 2 and pick up the bar before the next stitch,* repeat from * to * to the end of the needle (increases by 9 stitches per needle].

On the 2nd and 3rd needles, increase by picking up the bar between the 1st and 2nd stitches, then *knit 4 and pick up the bar before the next stitch,* repeat from * to * to the end of the needle (increases by 5 stitches per needle]. You should now have 108 stitches.

Mark the start of the round with a stitch marker and continue knitting in stocking stitch using the 6mm (US 10, UK 4) circular knitting needles.

When the piece measures 20cm (8in) from the cast-on edge, start decreasing by knitting together every 9th and 10th stitch. Decrease on every other round as follows: on the next decrease round, knit together every 8th and 9th stitch, on the following decrease round, knit together the 7th and 8th stitch. Continue in this way until only 9 stitches are left. (When there are too few stitches left to knit comfortably on the circular knitting needle, change to the 6mm (US 10, UK 4) double-pointed needles.)

Pull together the remaining 9 stitches firmly with a double yarn and secure the yarn. Darn in the yarn ends.

Cinderella

Ballet slippers

She shall go to the ball, or at least to the bath, in these sweet, cosy slippers. The trick here is to get the gathered toe right, making these felted shoes look elegant.

Sizes

UK shoe size 4–6/US shoe size 6–9.

Materials and needles

- Bulky wool yarn, suitable for felting: 100g (3½oz) in pink and 50g (1¾oz) in orange
- 6mm (US 10, UK 4) double-pointed needles or size needed to obtain the correct gauge
- 5mm (US H-8, UK 6) crochet hook
- Blunt-ended needle
- Stitch markers (or see the tip)
- Cable needle

Patterns

Garter stitch: working in rows, knit every row.
Stocking stitch: working in rounds, knit every round; working in rows, knit 1 row, purl 1 row, alternating.

Gauge

20 stitches and 26 rows worked in stocking stitch using 6mm (US 10, UK 4) knitting needles and 1 strand of yarn = 10 × 10cm (4 × 4in) before felting.

Instructions

These slippers are felted in the washing machine after knitting, which is why they are initially made in a larger size.

Sole

Cast on 10 stitches using 2 yarns, 1 in each colour together. Knit in garter-stitch rows. On row 2, increase 1 stitch on each side. After 25 garter ribs (50 rows), increase 1 stitch on each side, work 1 row straight and then on the next row increase by 1 stitch on each side again. Mark these increases on both sides with a stitch marker or length of contrasting yarn (see the tip).

When the piece measures 27cm (10¾in), cast off 2 stitches on each side, work 1 row straight then cast off another 2 stitches on each side.

When the piece measures 29cm (11½in), loosely cast off all the stitches.

Foot

Using pink yarn, pick up 115 stitches from all around the edge of the sole and divide evenly over 4 needles, with 2 needles on each side of each stitch marker (29 stitches on 3 needles and 28 stitches on the remaining needle). Working in rounds, knit 7cm (2¾in) in stocking stitch.

Continue working in shortened rows as follows: knit over the stitches of the tip of the toe (between the stitch markers) backwards and forwards in rows of stocking stitch, picking up and working one of the stitches on the adjacent holding needle at the start of a new row. On row 7 (right-side row), knit together the 32 stitches from the centre of the tip of the

foot as follows: *place 4 stitches on a cable needle behind the work parallel to the left needle. Knit together the next 4 stitches with the 4 stitches on the cable needle.*
Repeat from * to * another 3 times.
Knit 1 round in stocking stitch over all the stitches then loosely cast off all the stitches. Work both shoes in the same way.

Assembly

Darn in all the yarn ends.
Crochet around the edge of each slipper in double crochet (US single crochet) using orange yarn, crocheting 2 stitches together at a time at the tip of the foot between the stitch markers to accommodate the curve.
To felt, wash both shoes at 40 °C in the washing machine using detergent (you could also add 2 tennis balls to provide extra friction and encourage the felting process).
Before drying, put the slippers on and stretch them into shape. You may wish to stuff the slippers with paper and leave to dry.

Tip

If you do not have stitch markers available, you could use a piece of contrasting yarn instead – a cotton yarn in a different shade to the main yarn would be best. Place the yarn at the appropriate point. Once your slippers are finished, you can simply pull the yarn out again.

Hansel and Gretel

Hat and scarf

No need to worry about cold weather with this cosy duo. The scarf is very easy and gives you the chance to learn cabling, while the coordinating cabled hat features earflaps and a pompom.

Sizes

Fits a 54–57cm (21¼/22½in) head circumference.
The scarf is 220 × 20cm (86½ × 8in).

Materials and needles

- 500g (17½oz) of chunky/bulky yarn in brown
- 7mm (US 10½, UK 2) double-pointed needles (for the hat) or size needed to obtain the correct gauge
- 8mm (US 11, UK 0) knitting needles (for the scarf)
- 7mm (US K-10½, UK 2) crochet hook (for the hat)
- Cable needle
- Stitch holder
- Stitch marker
- Card for the pompom

- Blunt-ended needle
- Sharp, pointed scissors

Patterns

Seed stitch: *knit 1, purl 1,* repeat from * to * across right-side rows. On wrong-side rows, if you have an uneven number of stitches, work *knit 1, purl 1,* repeat from * to * to the end.

Cable pattern 1 (for the hat, multiple of 9 stitches): work following the chart, repeating the 6-row pattern.

Cable pattern 2 (for the scarf): work following the chart, repeating the 10-row pattern.

Cable pattern 1

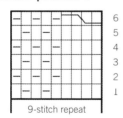

9-stitch repeat

☒ = selvedge
☐ = knit 1
⊟ = purl 1

= place 2 stitches on a cable needle in front of the work, knit 2, knit the stitches on the cable needle

= place 3 stitches on a cable needle in front of the work, knit 3, knit the stitches on the cable needle

Cable pattern 2

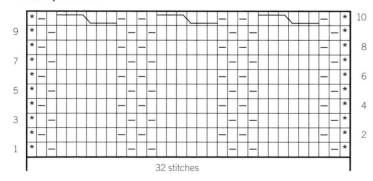

32 stitches

Gauge

12 stitches and 18 rows knit worked in cable pattern 1 using 7mm (US 10½, UK 2) knitting needles = 10 × 10cm (4 × 4in). The gauge for the scarf is not important as there is no need to worry about fit.

Instructions

Hat

Earflaps: cast on 5 stitches using 7mm (US 10½, UK 2) needles and knit in seed stitch.

On the 2nd, 4th, 6th and 8th rows, increase 1 stitch on each side and integrate into the design [13 stitches].

After 17 rows, put the 13 stitches on to the stitch holder.

Knit a 2nd earflap in the same way, but do not put the stitches on the stitch holder, rather cast on 23 stitches directly after the earflap by placing the yarn (like a loop) twisted over the needle and pull up.

Then knit the stitches of the 1st earflap in seed stitch and cast on a further 14 stitches [63 stitches].

Main part of the hat: close the work at the start of the 2nd earflap into a round, making sure that the stitches are not twisted, and mark the start of the round with a stitch marker.

Knit 1 round in seed stitch and then begin working in cable pattern 1.

When the piece measures 5cm (2in) from the start of the main part of the hat (total length of 14cm/5½in including earflaps), start decreasing. On the 1st decrease round, knit together both stitches before and after the cable so that the seed-stitch pattern is maintained in each repeat. Move the stitch marker at the start of the round to this point.

Knit a further 4cm (1½in) in cable pattern 1 and then purl together the 3 remaining seed stitches in each repeat. On the next round, work all stitches in the established pattern. On the next round knit 2 together across the stitches of the cables.

Knit 1 round in the pattern then cut off the end of the yarn, thread it through the remaining stitches, pull up tightly and finish off.

Assembly

Crochet around the edge of the hat with 1 round of double crochet (US single crochet), crocheting into every selvedge stitch of the earflaps.

Tassels: cut lengths of yarn and divide them into three groups of 5 lengths. Plait these three groups together, knotting one end to make a finished length of 20cm (8in) – you will need to experiment a little to see how long the yarn needs to be before you start plaiting. (You can also adjust the number of strands to make thicker or thinner tassels, as desired.) Make two tassels and sew one to the bottom of each earflap, with the knot at the free end. Trim the ends of the yarns to the same length, about 3cm (1¼in) below the knot.

Pompom: cut out two rings from card with an external diameter of 7cm (3in) and with a central hole with a 2cm (¾in) diameter. Place the rings on top of one another and bind evenly with wool until the hole in the middle is completely filled. Cut the bound wool between the card rings using the tip of a sharp pair of scissors. Thread a long piece of wool yarn between the card rings and tie the bound wool firmly with it. Carefully remove the card rings. Roll the pompom in your hand and cut off any yarns that stick out so that it forms an even, round shape. Sew the pompom firmly on to the hat using the tied yarn. Darn in all the yarn ends.

Scarf

Cast on 32 stitches using the 8mm (US 11, UK 0) needles and work in cable pattern 2 (1st row = wrong-side row). After about 220cm (86½in), 6 rows after the last cable, loosely cast off all the stitches – so that the scarf does not look too wide here, knit together both middle stitches in the cable, then cast off.

Assembly

Neaten the yarn ends. Stretch out the scarf, cover with damp towels and then quickly steam with an iron; leave to dry.

Alice in Wonderland

Cashmere sweater

This lightweight sweater is knitted in stocking stitch with a single cable detail. Its slim lines and low neckline are classically elegant, and the use of a luxury yarn gives added refinement.

Sizes

UK 6–8, 10–12 and 14–16/US 4–6, 8–10 and 12–14.
The details for the different sizes are separated by a forward slash. If there is no slash, then the details are applicable to all three sizes.

Materials and needles

- 100g (3½oz) of 4-ply/fingering luxury yarn in brown (the one used is 70% cashmere and 30% silk)
- 3mm (US 3, UK 11) circular knitting needles, 80cm (32in) and 60cm (24in) long, or size needed to obtain the correct gauge
- 4.5mm (US 7, UK 7) circular knitting needles, 80cm (32in) long
- Cable needle
- Blunt-ended needle
- Stitch markers

Patterns

Stocking stitch: working in rounds, knit every round; working in rows, knit 1 row, purl 1 row, alternating.

Gauge

24 stitches and 40 rows worked in stocking stitch using 3mm (US 3, UK 11) knitting needles = 10 × 10cm (4 × 4in).

Instructions

Back and front

The sweater is knitted in rounds as far as the neckline.
Cast on 180/196/220 stitches using the 4.5mm (US 7, UK 7) circular knitting needles and two yarns (this gives a strong, stretchy edge). Fasten off 1 yarn and continue knitting with the other. Purl 1 row then knit 1 row and close the work into a round, making sure that the stitches are not twisted. Mark the start of the round with a stitch marker then continue knitting in rounds in stocking stitch.
When the piece measures 32/32/34cm (12½/12½/13½in), change to the longer 3mm (US 3, UK 11) needles and mark

the centre of the Front section with another stitch marker. Knit 10 rounds in stocking stitch, but work the 6 stitches before the stitch marker as purl 2, knit 4 then work the 6 stitches after the marker as knit 4, purl 2.
On round 11, cable the middle 8 stitches as follows: place 4 stitches on a cable needle in front of the work, knit the next 4 stitches then knit the 4 stitches on the cable needle.
Knit the next 2 rounds in stocking stitch, working the central 12 stitches divided up as before with purl 2, knit 4, marker, knit 4, purl 2.
V-neckline: separate the work at the centre-front marker and complete the piece in rows, starting and finishing each row at the neck edge. Now shape the neckline by decreasing 1 stitch on every other row 8/8/10 times as follows: work 1 selvedge stitch, knit 3, purl 2, slip 1 purlwise, knit 1, pass the slipped stitch over. Continue knitting in stocking stitch until 8 stitches before the end of the row, knit 2 together, purl 2, knit 3, 1 selvedge stitch.
Armhole: when the piece measures 48/48/50cm (19/19/19¾in), 41 stitches

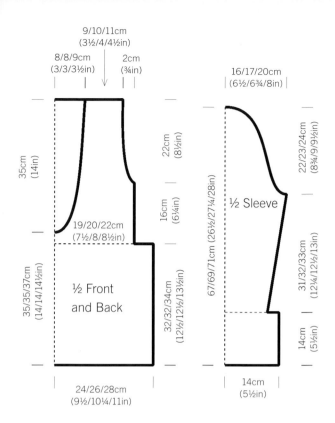

½ Front and Back

9/10/11cm
(3½/4/4½in)

8/8/9cm
(3/3/3½in)

2cm
(¾in)

35cm
(14in)

35/35/37cm
(14/14/14½in)

22cm
(8½in)

16cm
(6¼in)

19/20/22cm
(7½/8/8½in)

32/32/34cm
(12½/12½/13½in)

24/26/28cm
(9½/10¼/11in)

½ Sleeve

16/17/20cm
(6½/6¾/8in)

22/23/24cm
(8¾/9/9½in)

67/69/71cm (26½/27¼/28in)

31/32/33cm
(12¼/12½/13in)

14cm
(5½in)

14cm
(5½in)

before and after the neckline attach a stitch marker to mark the start of the armhole. From this point on, continue knitting the Back and both the Front pieces separately between these markers. For all pieces, cast off 3 stitches on each side, work one row straight, then cast off 2 stitches on each side, work 1 row straight and then on the next 2 alternate rows cast off 1 stitch on each side. When the piece measures 70/70/72cm (27½/27½/28½in), loosely cast off all the stitches.

Sleeve

Cast on 48/54/64 stitches with the 4.5mm (US 7, UK 7) circular needles and knit in rows of stocking stitch (1st row = wrong-side row with purl stitches). When the piece measures 14cm (5½in) change, to 3mm (US 3, UK 11) needles. When the piece measures 16/18/18cm (6¼/7/7in) increase 1 stitch on each side. Then increase by 1 stitch every 6th row 13/13/15 times on both sides [78/82/94 stitches].

When the piece measures 45/46/47cm (17¾/18/18½in), start decreasing for the sleeve head, by casting off 4/6/6 stitches on each side. Work one row straight and then on alternate rows cast off 3 stitches once/3 stitches once/two stitches twice and then 1 stitch 4/5/6 times. Knit 10 rows in straight stocking stitch. Then, on alternate rows, decrease 1 stitch 7 times on each side then cast off 2 stitches twice and then 4 stitches twice on each side. On the next row, loosely cast off the remaining stitches. Work the second sleeve in the same way.

Assembly

Carefully stretch out all the pieces, cover with a damp cloth and leave to dry. Close the shoulder and sleeve seams and insert the sleeves. Darn in all the yarn ends.

Tom Thumb

Striped toddler's sweater

This striped sweater can be made without having to follow a difficult pattern. Even beginners can attempt this one. You just need to ensure that you change colours at the right time.

Sizes

9–12 months and 18–24 months. The details for the different sizes are separated by a forward slash. If there is no slash, then the details are applicable to both sizes.

Materials and needles

- Cotton yarn in a baby weight: 100/150g (3½/5¼oz) each in green and white
- 3mm (US 3, UK 11) knitting needles or size needed to obtain the correct gauge
- Blunt-ended needle
- 3 press studs

Patterns

Ribbing: *knit 2, purl 2,* repeat from * to * across the row. On wrong-side rows, work all stitches as they appear.

Stocking stitch: knit right-side rows, purl wrong-side rows.

Stripes: *work 12 rows in green then 12 rows in white*. Repeat from * to *.

Gauge

24 stitches and 32 rows worked in stocking stitch using 3mm (US 3, UK 11) knitting needles = 10 × 10cm (4 × 4in).

Instructions

Front

Cast on 58/68 stitches in green and knit 2cm (¾in) in ribbing.

Continue knitting in stocking stitch, working in stripes.

Neckline: when the piece measures 25.5/27.5cm (10/10¾in) from the cast-on edge, cast off the middle 24 stitches and finish both sides separately, making the neck decreases as follows on every other row: on the side of the neckline, cast off another 2 stitches once and then 1 stitch 3 times.

Right shoulder: when the piece measures 28/30cm (11/12in) from the cast-on edge, cast off the remaining 15/17 stitches.

Left shoulder: when the piece measures 28/30cm (11/12in) from the cast-on edge, knit another 2cm (¾in) on the remaining 15/17 stitches in ribbing (press-stud welt), then cast off all the stitches.

Back

Cast on 58/68 stitches in green and knit 2cm (¾in) in ribbing.

Continue knitting in stocking stitch, working in stripes.

When the piece measures 28/30cm (11/12in) from the cast-on edge, cast off the stitches.

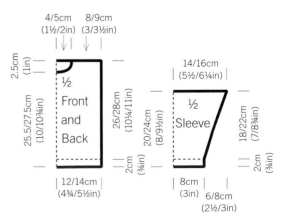

Sleeve

Cast on 42 stitches and knit 2cm (¾in) in ribbing.

Continue knitting in stocking stitch, working in stripes.

When the piece measures 4cm (1½in), increase 1 stitch on each side then every 4/3 rows increase by 1 stitch on each side 12/16 times.

When the piece measures 20/24cm (8/9½in) from the cast-on edge, loosely cast off all the stitches.

Work the second sleeve in the same way.

Assembly

Stretch out all the pieces according to the pattern, dampen and leave to dry. Close the right shoulder seam and the side seams.

Neckline trim: on the right side of the work and starting at the top corner of the ribbing at the left shoulder, pick up 114/120 stitches from the neckline and work in ribbing.

Row 6 (wrong-side row): *purl 2, knit 2 together *, repeat from * to *, ending with purl 2.

Row 7 (right-side row): *knit 2, purl 1; repeat from * to *, ending with knit 2.

Rows 8–9: continue working all stitches in the ribbing pattern established.

On the next row, loosely cast off all the stitches.

Insert 3 press studs in the ribbing at the left shoulder, evenly spaced and on the corresponding edge of the Back piece that lies underneath. Darn in all the yarn ends.

The Rose Queen

Rose embellishment

You could wear this rose as an accessory on a jacket lapel or pocket. Several roses would also look good as a table decoration or on a hat or bag.

Materials and needles

- Remnants of mohair yarn
- 3.5mm (US 4, UK 10) knitting needles or size needed to obtain the correct gauge
- Blunt-ended needle

Patterns

Stocking stitch: knit right-side rows, purl wrong-side rows.

Increase (increase 1 stitch): lift the bar of yarn between the stitch just knitted and the next stitch on to the left needle and knit through the back loop.

Gauge

20 stitches and 27 rows worked in stocking stitch using 3.5mm (US 4, UK 10) knitting needles = 10 × 10cm (4 × 4in).

Instructions

Cast on 20 stitches and knit in stocking stitch as follows:

Row 1 (wrong side): purl.
Row 2 (right side): ˄ knit 1, increase 1,˄ repeat from * to * ending with knit 1 [39 stitches].
Row 3: purl.
Row 4: * knit 2, increase 1; repeat from * to *, ending with knit 1 [58 stitches].
Row 5: purl.

Row 6: *knit 4, increase 1; repeat from * to *, ending with knit 2 [72 stitches].
Rows 7–11: work in stocking stitch. Loosely cast off all stitches purlwise.

Assembly

Roll up the knitted strip, starting from one end, and fix it by hand at the cast-on edge using the ends of the yarn.

Thumbelina

Little girl's coat

Worked in seed stitch for a wonderfully textured finish and with front pleats for extra style and fullness, this little girl's dress coat is a project that you will fall in love with.

Sizes

12–18 months and 2–3 years.
The details for the different sizes are separated by a forward slash. If there is no slash, then the details are applicable to both sizes.

Materials and needles

- 500/550g (17½/19½in) of double-knitting/worsted weight merino wool in royal blue
- 4.5mm (US 7, UK 7) knitting needles or size needed to obtain the correct gauge
- 4 or 5mm (US G-6, UK 8 or US H-8, UK 6) crochet hook
- 2 cable needles
- 3 stitch holders
- Blunt-ended needle
- 4 buttons in dark blue, 30mm (1¼in) in diameter

Patterns

Seed stitch: *knit 1, purl 1,* repeat from * to * across right-side rows. On wrong-side rows, if you have an even number of stitches, work *purl 1, knit 1,* repeat from * to * to the end.
Reverse stocking stitch (individual stitches for the inverted pleat): purl on right-side rows, knit on wrong-side rows.

Gauge

19 stitches and 26 rows worked in in seed stitch using 4.5mm (US 7, UK 7) knitting needles = 10 × 10cm (4 × 4in).

Instructions

Back

Cast on 80/90 stitches and knit 20/21cm (8/8¼in) in seed stitch.
Next row (right-side row): work 1 selvedge stitch, 30 seed stitches, knit 3 together 6/9 times, work 30 seed stitches, 1 selvedge stitch [68/72 stitches].
Continue knitting in seed stitch until the piece measures 26/28cm (10¼/11in) from the cast-on edge.

Armholes: cast off on alternate rows, 3 stitches once, then 2 stitches once and then 1 stitch 3 times on both sides [52/56 stitches].
Continue knitting in seed stitch until the piece measures 39/42cm (15½/16½in).
Neckline: on the following right-side row, cast off the middle 14 stitches and then complete each side separately, casting off on the neck edge of alternate rows first 2 stitches and then 1 stitch. When the piece measures 41/43cm (16/17in), casl off the remaining stitches.

Left Front (as worn)

Both Front pieces of the coat are made from a total of 3 pieces: inverted pleat, front section and side section.
Inverted pleat: Cast on 28 stitches and work as follows for 15/17cm (6/6¾in): 1 selvedge stitch, 5 seed stitches, 1 reverse stocking stitch (i.e. purl on right-side rows, knit on wrong-side rows), 14 seed stitches, 1 reverse stocking stitch, 5 seed stitches 1 selvedge stitch.
On the next row (right-side row) form the pleat as follows: work 1 selvedge stitch then 5 seed stitches, place these

6 stitches on a cable needle parallel and in front of the work and *knit together 1 stitch from the cable needle with 1 stitch from the left needle, repeating the process from * until you have used up all the stitches on the cable needle.

Continue knitting in the established pattern until 12 stitches before the end of the row. Place the last 6 stitches on a cable needle parallel and in front of the work and *knit together 1 stitch of the cable needle with 1 stitch of the left needle, repeating the process from * until you have used up the remaining stitches. The pleat should now be formed with the two side edges facing inwards and parallel near the centre.

Put all the stitches on a stitch holder.

Front section: Cast on 27 stitches and knit 15/17cm (6/6¾in) in seed stitch. Put all the stitches on a stitch holder.

Side section: Cast on 15/18 stitches and knit 15/17cm (6/6¾in) in seed stitch. Put all stitches on a stitch holder.

Now put the 3 parts together as follows: knit 8/11 stitches from the side section in seed stitch. Put the stitches of the inverted pleat on to a cable needle (the opening of the pleat faces forward). Place the cable needle parallel behind the work and knit together the first 7 stitches of the cable needle with the remaining 7 stitches of the side section.

Put the stitches of the front section on a cable needle and place this 2nd cable needle parallel in front of the cable needle with the stitches of the inverted pleat. Knit together the first 7 stitches of the front section with the remaining 7 stitches of the inverted pleat.

Knit the remaining 20 stitches of the front section in seed stitch [42/45 stitches in total for the Front].

Continue knitting in seed stitch. When the piece measures 20/22cm (8/8¾in), work 2 buttonholes on a wrong-side row as follows: work 1 selvedge stitch, 3 seed stitches, cast off 3 stitches (1st buttonhole), 14 seed

stitches, cast off 3 stitches (2nd buttonhole). Continue knitting in seed stitch until the end of the row. On the following right-side row, cast on 3 stitches over the cast-off stitches.

When the piece measures 26/28cm (10¼/11in), work the armhole as for the Back.

When the piece measures 30cm (12in) work another 2 buttonholes.

When the piece measures 36/39cm (14/15½in), cast off 20 stitches on the side of the neckline then, on alternate rows cast off from the neck edge 2 stitches once and then 1 stitch once.

When the piece measures 39/42cm (15½/16½in), cast off.

Right Front

Work as for the Left Front, but without working the buttonholes.

Sleeves (make 2)

Cast on 38 stitches and knit in seed stitch. When the piece measures 8cm (3in), increase by 1 stitch on each side and then increase 1 stitch on each side of every 6th row 5/6 times, maintaining the stitch pattern.

When the piece measures 21/22cm (8¼/8¾in), cast off as follows on each side of alternate rows: 3 stitches once, 2 stitches once and 1 stitch 3/4 times.

When the piece measures 26/28cm (10¼/11in), knit the next right-side row as follows: knit 11 stitches in seed stitch, knit 2 together 6 times, knit 11 stitches in seed stitch.

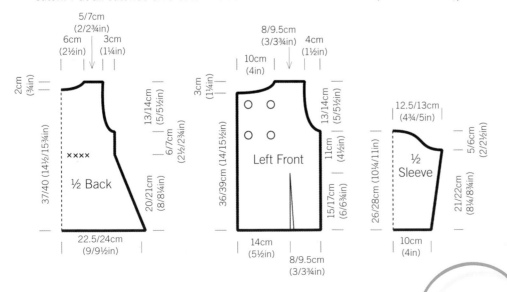

On the following (wrong-side) row, cast off all stitches.
Work the second sleeve in the same way.

Assembly

Crochet together the edges of the inverted pleat pieces with those of the corresponding side and front sections using chain stitch.
Stretch out all the pieces, dampen them and leave to dry.
Close the shoulder, side and sleeve seams and insert the sleeves.
Collar: 14 stitches back from the front edge of the neckline on the left side of the work, pick up 85 stitches from the neckline and work in seed stitch for 8 rows. On the 9th row, alternating every 8th and 9th stitch, increase 3 stitches and integrate into the seed-stitch pattern [103 stitches]. When the collar is 6cm (2½in), loosely cast off all the stitches.
Darn in all the yarn ends.
Sew the buttons to the Right Front piece using knitting yarn, aligning them with the buttonholes.

Tip

Seed stitch looks the same on the front and back of the work. You can only tell the difference by the cast-on row. When you are putting the pieces together, make sure that have the right piece the right way round.

Extra tips

The pieces for this model are knitted in rows but if you use a circular knitting needle for this, still knitting in rows, you will make the work a lot easier because the weight of the knitting rests in your lap and is not continually putting a strain on your wrists. A circular needle used this way also makes it easier to work the inverted pleat pieces.

If you do not have enough stitch holders in your knitting basket for this model, you can thread the stitches on to a piece of smooth yarn and put them back on to the knitting needle again when you need them. It is best to use a cotton yarn in a contrasting colour that is not too thin, so that you are easily able to recognise the stitches when you are transferring them.

Snow White and Rose Red

Wrapover cardigan

This wrapover top is a challenge due to the 2-count ribbing but the clever construction means that there are no seams to join at the end. The two-colour work gives the cardigan a wonderful glowing finish.

Sizes

UK 8–12 and 14–16/US 6–10 and 12–14.
The details for the different sizes are separated by a forward slash. If there is no slash, then the details are applicable to both sizes.

Materials and needles

- 75g (3oz) of good-quality mohair yarn in each of very pale pink and mid pink or in your preferred colours
- 6mm (US 10, UK 4) circular knitting needles, 80cm (31½in) and 60cm (24in) long, or size needed to obtain the correct gauge
- Blunt-ended needle
- Stitch holder
- Stitch marker

Patterns

Ribbing: *knit 1, purl 1,* repeat from * to * to end of round. As you are knitting on circular needles, there is no wrong-side row.

Two-toned pattern: make sure you practice the pattern first, ideally using two cotton yarns, as they are easier to separate again if you need to unravel, unlike mohair.

Row 1 (dark yarn): work 1 selvedge stitch, *knit 1, slip 1 purlwise with yarn over,* repeat from * to * until 1 stitch before the end of the row; place the yarn in front of the work and slip the last stitch.

Row 2 (light yarn): do not turn the work but push all the stitches to the other end of the needle and continue working with the light yarn. Slip the selvedge stitch, *slip 1 purlwise with yarn over, purl together the next stitch and the dark yarn over of the previous row,* repeat from * to * until 1 stitch before the end of the row; slip the last stitch (yarn in front of the work). Turn the work.

Row 3 (dark yarn): *slip 1 purlwise with yarn over, purl the next stitch and the light yarn over of the previous row together,* repeat from * to * until 1 stitch before the end of the row; slip the last stitch (yarn in front of the work).

Row 4 (light yarn): do not turn the work but push all the stitches to the other end of the needle and continue working with the light yarn. Slip the selvedge stitch, *knit the next stitch with the dark yarn over of the previous row, slip 1 purlwise with yarn over,* repeat from * to * to the end. Repeat this 4-row pattern.

Gauge

14 stitches and 30 rows worked in the two-toned pattern using 6mm (US 10, UK 4) knitting needles = 10 × 10cm (4 × 4in).

Instructions

Using the longer circular needles, cast on 56 stitches with the light and dark yarns together. Work in the two-toned pattern (starting with the dark yarn; see above). Remember that after the 1st row you do not turn the work, but push all the stitches to the other end of the needle and continue working with the light yarn.

Sleeves (make 2)

Using the shorter circular needles, pick up 40 stitches with the light and dark yarns together from one armhole on the dark side of the knitted piece and close the work into a round. Mark the start of the round with a stitch marker.

Round 1 (dark yarn): *purl 1, knit 1,* repeat from * to * to the end of the round.

Round 2 (dark yarn): *for the stitch on the left, slip 1 purlwise with yarn over, knit 1,* repeat from * to * to the end of the round.

Round 3 (light yarn): (light yarn): *knit the slip stitch purlwise with the yarn over, for the stitch on the right slip 1 knitwise with yarn over,* repeat from * to * to the end of the round.

Repeat rounds 2 and 3 until the piece measures 48cm (19in).

Work in ribbing using both colours parallel.

When the ribbing measures 12cm (5in), loosely cast off all the stitches.

Work the second sleeve in the same way. Darn in all the yarn ends to finish.

1st armhole: when the piece measures 98/100cm (38½/39½in), end with 1 row in the dark colour. Knit 13 stitches using the light yarn and put these stitches on the stitch holder, cast off the next 16 stitches then knit 27 stitches. Knit 6cm (2½in) in the two-tone pattern over these 27 stitches. Cast on 16 stitches over the ones previously cast off for the armhole, and end the row with the 13 stitches on the stitch holder.

2nd armhole: knit 22/25cm (8¾/10in) in the two-toned pattern over all the stitches. Make the 2nd armhole as described above.

Knit another 98/100cm (38½/39½in) in the two-toned pattern over all the stitches. Loosely cast off all stitches.

Puss in Boots

Knee-high socks

Very fashionable and easy to knit, these socks look great peaking out of boots. Make either the colourfully striped socks or the plain socks with a decorative top band. The instructions for the striped socks are given here. For instructions on making the grey socks, see page 62.

Sizes

UK shoe size 3.5–9/US shoe size 5.5–11. (See the table on page 65 for details of individual sizes.)

Materials and needles

- 200g (7oz) of self-striping sock yarn in red-pink-yellow-purple
- Waste yarn for the cast-on
- 3mm (US 3, UK 11) circular knitting needle (the length is unimportant because this is only used for casting on)
- 2.5mm (US 1, UK 13) double-pointed needles, or size needed to obtain the correct gauge
- Blunt-ended needle
- Stitch marker

Patterns

Ribbing: *knit 1, purl 1,* repeat from * to * to end of round. As you are knitting in rounds, there is no wrong-side row.

Stocking stitch: in rounds, knit all stitches; in rows (heel cap), knit right-side rows, purl wrong-side rows.

Gauge

30 stitches and 42 rows worked in stocking stitch using 2.5mm (US 1, UK 13) knitting needles = 10 × 10cm (4 × 4in).

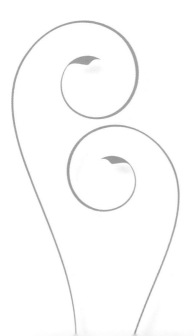

Instructions for the striped socks

Cuff

As a stretchy top band is particularly important for knee-high socks – you need to be able to get them on, but you also want them to stay up – start with an Italian cast-on stitch (or you can use any stretchy cast-on method of your choice): cast on half the number of stitches required for the desired size (see the table on page 65) using waste yarn in a contrasting colour and the circular knitting needles. Purl 1 (wrong-side) row. Using the self-striping yarn and the double-pointed needles continue working as follows:

Round 1: * knit 1, yarn over,* repeat from * to * to the end of the round, dividing up the stitches equally over the 4 needles as instructed in the table on page 65.

Round 2: *slip the knit stitch of the previous round purlwise (yarn behind the work), bring the yarn forward (as if to purl),* repeat from * to * to the end of the round.

Round 3: * knit the knit stitch, slip the purl stitch purlwise (yarn in front of

work),* repeat from * to * to the end of the round.

Round 4: : *slip the knit stitch purlwise (yarn behind the work), purl the purl stitch,* repeat from * to * to the end of the round.

From round 5 onwards, work in the knit 1, purl 1 ribbing pattern. Mark the beginning/end of each round at the centre back with a stitch marker.

Leg

When the cuff measures 3cm (1¼in), begin working in stocking stitch.

Work the decrease for the calf in the centre back according to the table as follows:

1st needle: knit 1, slip 1, knit 1, pass the slipped stitch over, knit to the end of the needle.

2nd and 3rd needle: knit.

4th needle: knit until 3 stitches before the end of the needle, knit 2 together, knit 1.

Knit the leg to the stated length (see the table on page 65) then start the heel.

Heel

Knit 28 or 30 rows over the stitches of the 1st and 4th needles (see table). Then divide up the stitches into 3 sections (see table) and knit the heel cap as follows: on the next right-side row, knit as far as the last stitch of the 2nd section, *slip the last stitch as if to knit, and also slip the following stitch (1st stitch of the 3rd section). Turn the work. Purl together both slipped stitches, then purl all the stitches of the middle section as far as the last stitch. Slip this stitch as if to knit, and also slip the next stitch (1st stitch of the final section) and turn the work. Knit both slipped stitches together. Knit the following stitches of the middle section as far as the last stitch.* Continue in this way, repeating from * to *, until all the stitches of both outer sections have been worked.

Foot

Knit in rounds over all the stitches again. Divide the cap stitches on to 2 needles (1st and 4th needles). With the 1st needle, pick up 1 stitch from every selvedge stitch of the left edge of the heel, cast on 1 and knit through the back loop between the 1st and 2nd needles. Knit the stitches of the 2nd and 3rd needles. Between the 3rd and 4th needles, cast on 1 and knit through the back loop. Pick up 1 stitch from every selvedge stitch of the right edge of the heel. Knit the remaining stitches of the 4th needle (cap stitch) in stocking stitch. On the 1st and 4th needles there are now more stitches than on the 2nd and 3rd needles. These stitches are cast off again for the gusset as follows: for the 1st needle, knit together the second-last and third-to-last stitches; for the 4th needle, knit the 1st stitch, slip the 2nd stitch, knit the 3rd stitch and pass the slipped stitch over. Repeat this decreasing in every 3rd round, until the original number of stitches is reached again for all 4 needles. Knit the foot in stocking stitch to the length given in the table.

Toe

For the toe, decrease according to the table as follows: knit the stitches of the 1st and 3rd needles as far as the last 3 stitches, knit 2 together, knit the last stitch. For the 2nd and 4th needles, knit the 1st stitch, slip the following stitch, knit 1 stitch, pass the slipped stitch over. Repeat this decreasing at the stated intervals (see the table on page 65), until there are only 8 stitches left. Pull these stitches tightly together with a double yarn and secure the end. Darn in the ends.

Work the second sock in the same way.

Tip

Socks are very easy to knit using short, sock knitting needles made from bamboo: they are light and easy to use, due to their length. They feel nice and warm and the yarn slides well over the natural material. Make sure you use high-quality ones, as poorer quality bamboo needles may have wood fibres sticking out of them, which can catch on the yarn.

Socks with a decorative top band

These knee-high socks look great with fashionable boots. Just leave the trim peeking out of the top of the boot to achieve the perfect, young-at-heart look.

Sizes
Shoe size 3.5/4 to 8/9.
(See the table on page 65 for details of individual sizes).

Materials and needles
- 100g (3½oz) of sock yarn in mid-grey
- 2.5mm (US 1, UK 13) and 3mm (US 3, UK 11) double-pointed needles
- Cable needle
- 2.5mm (US B-1, UK 12) crochet hook
- Blunt-ended needle
- Stitch marker

Patterns
Ribbing: working in rounds,* knit 1, purl 1,* repeat from * to *.
Stocking stitch: in rounds, knit every round.
Trim (number of stitches divisible by 5):
Round 1–2: *knit 4, purl 1,* repeat from * to * to the end of the round.
Round 3: *knit 3, yarn over, knit 1, yarn over, purl 1,* repeat from * to * to the end of the round.
Round 4: *place 3 stitches on a cable needle behind the work, drop the first yarn over (from round 3), knit the next stitch, drop the second yarn over then knit the 3 stitches from the cable needle, purl 1, * repeat from * to * to the end of the round.
Repeat these 4 rounds.

Gauge
30 stitches and 42 rounds worked in stocking stitch using 2.5mm (US 1, UK 13) knitting needles = 10 × 10cm (4 × 4in).

Instructions for the grey socks
The decorative top band is added at the end. To begin, use waste yarn in a contrasting colour to provisionally cast on with the number of stitches required for your size (see the table on page 65). Using the grey yarn, knit using the 2.5mm (US 1, UK 13) knitting needles, dividing the stitches equally over 4 needles, and close the work into a round. Mark the beginning/end of each round at the centre back with a stitch marker. Knit 3cm (1¼in) in the ribbing pattern.

Leg
Begin knitting in stocking stitch. Work the decrease for the calf in the centre back according to the table as follows:
1st needle: knit 1, slip 1, knit 1, pass the slipped stitch over, knit to the end of the needle.
2nd and 3rd needles: knit.
4th needle: knit to 3 stitches before the end of the needle, knit 2 together, knit 1. Continue knitting the leg to the stated length (see the table on page 65), then start the heel.

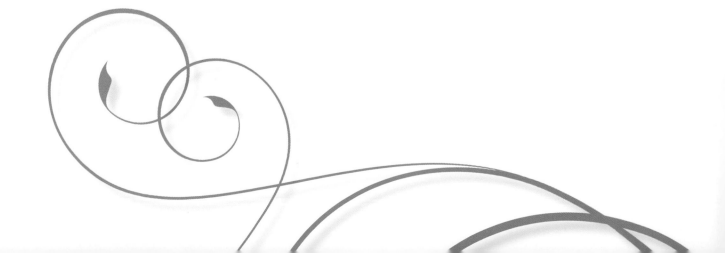

63

Heel

Knit 28 or 30 rows over the stitches of the 1st and 4th needles (see table). Then divide up the stitches into 3 sections (see table) and knit the heel cap as follows: on the next right-side row, knit as far as the last stitch of the 2nd section, *slip the last stitch as if to knit, and also slip the following stitch (1st stitch of the 3rd section). Turn the work. Purl together both slipped stitches, then purl all the stitches of the middle section as far as the last stitch. Slip this stitch as if to knit, and also slip the next stitch (1st stitch of the outer section) as if to knit and turn the work. Knit both slipped stitches together. Knit the following stitches of the middle section as far as the last stitch.* Continue repeating from * to * until all the stitches of both outer sections have been worked.

Foot

Knit in rounds over all the stitches again. Divide the cap stitches on to 2 needles (1st and 4th needles). With the 1st needle, pick up 1 stitch from every selvedge stitch of the left edge of the heel, cast on 1 and knit through the back loop between the 1st and 2nd needles. Knit the stitches of the 2nd and 3rd needles. Between the 3rd and 4th needles, cast on 1 and knit through the back loop. Pick up 1 stitch from every selvedge stitch of the right edge of the heel. Knit the remaining stitches of the 4th needle (cap stitch) in stocking stitch. On the 1st and 4th needles there are now more stitches than on the 2nd and 3rd needles. These stitches are cast off again for the gusset as follows: for the 1st needle, knit together the second- and third-to-last stitch; for the 4th needle, knit the 1st stitch, slip the 2nd stitch, knit the 3rd stitch and pass the slipped stitch over. Repeat this decrease in every 3rd round until the original number of stitches is reached again for all 4 needles. Knit the foot in stocking stitch to the length given in the table.

Trim

For the toe, decrease according to the table as follows: knit the stitches of the 1st and 3rd needles as far as the last 3 stitches, knit 2 together, knit the last stitch. For the 2nd and 4th needles, knit the 1st stitch, slip the following stitch, knit 1, pass the slipped stitch over. Repeat this decreasing at the stated intervals (see table), until there are only 8 stitches left. Pull these stitches tightly together with a double yarn and secure the end. Darn in the ends.

Trim

Turn the sock wrong side out. Carefully remove the chain stitch in the contrasting waste yarn and divide the provisional stitches over 4 needles. Knit 1 round. Pick up the bar after the 1st stitch of the 1st needle and knit through the back loop. Repeat in front of the last stitch of the 4th needle.

In the 2nd round, start the trim pattern. (Note: after the first 4 stitches and before the last 4 stitches of the round, purl 2.) Repeat the 4-round trim pattern 4 times, then repeat the 1st round another 3 times. On the following round, cast off all the stitches as loosely as possible using 3mm (US 3, UK 11) knitting needles. Work the second sock in the same way.

Knee-high socks table

Shoe size	3.5–4.5 (US 5.5–6.5)	5–6 (US 7–8)	6.5–7.5 (US 8.5–9.5)	8/9 (US 10–11)
Cast on / stitches per needle	76/19	80/20	64/21	88/22
Decrease for the calf (on 1st and 4th needles)				
1st decrease after	14cm (5½in)	14cm (5½in)	16cm (6¼in)	16cm (6¼in)
On every 8th round	2 times	2 times	2 times	2 times
On every 6th round	2 times	2 times	2 times	2 times
On every 4th round	3 times	5 times	5 times	7 times
Remaining stitches per needle	15	15	16	16
Leg height	34cm (13½in)	36cm (14¼in)	38cm (15in)	40cm (15¾in)
Heel				
Number of stitches for heel width	30	30	32	32
Number of rows for heel height	28	28	30	30
Number of stitches for cap	10/10/10	10/10/10	10/12/10	10/12/10
Cast-on stitches on both sides	15	15	16	16
Foot				
Length of foot to start of toe	18.5cm	20cm	21cm	22cm
Toe (decrease)				
1st decrease in the 4th round	1 time	1 time	1 time	1 time
On every 3rd round	2 times	2 times	2 times	2 times
On every other round	3 times	3 times	3 times	3 times
On every round	6 times	6 times	7 times	7 times
Total foot length	23.5cm (9¼in)	25cm (10in)	26.5cm (10½in)	27.5cm (10¾in)

Jack and the Beanstalk

Child's sweater

This sweater is a real classic for our little ones. Cables might look difficult, but they are only twisted stitches, and are very easy to work with a cable needle.

Sizes

12–18 months and 2–3 years.
The details for the different sizes are separated by a forward slash. If there is no slash, then the details are applicable to both sizes.

Materials and needles

- 200/250g (7/9oz) of double-knitting/ worsted weight merino wool in natural white
- 4.5mm (US 7, UK 7) and 5mm (US 8, UK 6) knitting needles
- Cable needle
- Blunt-ended needle
- 3 white buttons, 2cm (¾in) in diameter

Patterns

Cable pattern: work following the chart. The chart shows only the right-side rows; work the stitches on the wrong-side rows as they appear. The selvedge stitches are not shown.
Repeat the 8-row pattern.
Ribbing: *knit 2, purl 2,* repeat from * to * to the end of the row. Work all stitches on the wrong-side rows as they appear.

Gauge

18 stitches and 27 rows worked in ribbing using 4.5mm (US 7, UK 7) knitting needles = 10 × 10cm (4 × 4in) when slightly stretched.

Instructions

Front

Cast on 56/66 stitches using the 4.5mm (US 7, UK 7) needles and knit 4cm (1½in) in ribbing. Increase 1 stitch on the last wrong-side row [57/67 stitches]. Continue knitting as follows:
Size 12–18 months: change to 5mm (US 8, UK 6) knitting needles and work in the cable pattern, following the chart. Start as shown, beginning and ending every row with 1 selvedge stitch.
Size 2–3 years: change to 5mm (US 8, UK 6) knitting needles. Start with a selvedge stitch, knit 4 then work in the cable pattern, following the chart, ending with knit 4, 1 selvedge stitch.

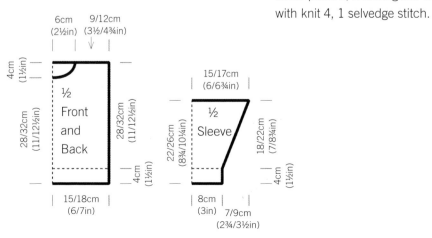

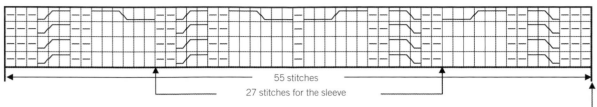

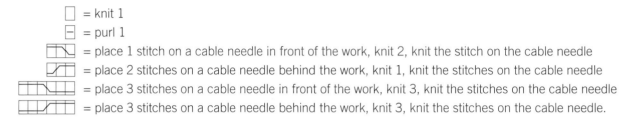

55 stitches

27 stitches for the sleeve

Start for size 12–18 months
Add 4 stitches each end
for size 2–3 years

Only the right-side rows are shown; knit the stitches on the wrong-side rows as they appear.
The selvedge stitches must also be worked.

☐ = knit 1

– = purl 1

= place 1 stitch on a cable needle in front of the work, knit 2, knit the stitch on the cable needle

= place 2 stitches on a cable needle behind the work, knit 1, knit the stitches on the cable needle

= place 3 stitches on a cable needle in front of the work, knit 3, knit the stitches on the cable needle

= place 3 stitches on a cable needle behind the work, knit 3, knit the stitches on the cable needle.

Continue knitting in the cable pattern for the relevant size.

Neckline: when the piece measures 28/32cm (11/12½in) from the cast-on edge, cast off the middle 13 stitches and finish each side separately. On the neck edge, cast off 2 stitches and then on alternate rows cast off a further 1 stitch 4 times.

When the piece measures 32/36cm (12½/14¼in), loosely cast off all the stitches.

Back

Work as for the Front but without casting off for the neckline. When the piece measures 32/36cm (12½/14¼in), loosely cast off all the stitches.

Sleeves (makes 2)

Cast on 30 stitches using the 4.5mm (US 7, UK 7) knitting needles and knit 4cm (1½in) in ribbing. On the last wrong-side row, increase by 1 stitch [31 stitches]. Change to 5mm (US 8, UK 6) knitting needles and begin working in the cable pattern, following the chart (start at the arrow in the pattern).

When the piece measures 6/5cm (2½/2in), start increasing for the slanted sleeve edges: increase by 1 stitch on each edge, then increase by 1 stitch every 4th row 12/13 times on each edge. Continue knitting in the cable pattern. When the piece measures 22/26cm (8¾/10¼in), loosely cast off all the stitches.
Work the second sleeve in the same way.

Assembly

Stretch out all the pieces according to the pattern, dampen and leave to dry. Close the left shoulder seam and the side seams. For the round neck trim, pick up 100 stitches from the neckline on the right side of the work using the 4.5mm (US 7, UK 7) knitting needles and work in the ribbing pattern. When the ribbing band measures 3cm (1¼in), loosely cast off all the stitches on a right-side row, working in the ribbing pattern.

Cast on 21 stitches from the cast-off edge of the right shoulder of the Front and work in the ribbing pattern. On the 5th row, work 3 buttonholes over 2 stitches each: the 1st buttonhole after 4 stitches, the two others at a distance of 3 stitches apart. Do this by casting off 2 stitches for each buttonhole and then casting on 2 new stitches on the following row over the cast-off stitches. After a total of 10 rows of ribbing, loosely cast off all the stitches. Darn in all the yarn ends. Sew the buttons on to the right shoulder of the Back to correspond with the buttonholes.

Valiant Little Tailor

Handbag

This handbag is perfect for carrying everything you need. You can wear it simply as it is or decorate it with knitted flowers or beads.

Size

Approximately 29 × 23cm (11½ × 9in).

Materials and needles

- 4-ply/sportweight cotton or cotton-blend yarn: 150g (5½oz) of brown and 100g (3½oz) in lime green
- 3mm (US 3, UK 11) circular knitting needle or size needed to obtain gauge
- 3mm (US C-2, UK 11) crochet hook
- Tacking thread
- Blunt-ended needle
- Sewing machine, optional

Patterns

Stocking stitch: knit right-side rows, purl wrong-side rows; in rounds, knit every round.

Gauge

20 stitches and 32 rows worked in stocking stitch using 3mm (US 3, UK 11) knitting needles = 10 × 10cm (4 × 4in).

Instructions

Strap and Sides

Cast on 262 stitches in brown and purl 1 row.

Knit 1 row and close the work into a round at the end of the row, making sure the stitches are not twisted.

Work in stocking stitch for 16cm (6¼in) and then loosely cast off all the stitches.

Front

Cast on 22 stitches in lime green and knit in stocking stitch. Make the following increases on every other row on each side: 4 stitches twice, then 3 stitches once and then 1 stitch twice. Work 3 rows straight and on the next row increase by 2 stitches on both sides, then increase 1 stitch on each side on every 6th row 8 times [68 stitches]. **

After the last increase, knit another 5cm (2in) in stocking stitch. Loosely cast off all stitches.

Back with flap

Work as for the Front as far as **.

After the last increase, knit another 14cm (5½in) in stocking stitch then decrease the stitches as follows for the flap: on the 6th and 7th rows, cast off 1 stitch on each side, work 3 rows straight and on the next row cast off 1 stitch on each side. Then on every other row on each side, cast off 1 stitch twice, then 3 stitches once and then 4 stitches twice. Work 1 row straight and on the next row loosely cast off all the stitches [68 stitches].

Assembly

Stretch out all the pieces, wrong side uppermost, and lightly moisten them beneath a damp cloth. Place the Front and Back pieces exactly opposite each other in the ring for the Strap and Sides, tack and then sew in place using the sewing machine.

Crochet around the edge of the flap with double crochet (US single crochet). Fold in the outside edges of the strap towards the middle and sew together. Darn in all the yarn ends.

Tip

When casting on so many stitches for the strap and side strips, we recommend that you knit a wrong-side row after the cast-on row and then close the work into a round. That way, you are better able to check that all the stitches are actually laying in the same direction when closed into a round and have not been twisted.

Rapunzel

Knitted dress

Long cables run the length of the dress, tapering off at the top, so that the skirt falls nice and loosely. Study the pattern first before you begin.

Sizes

UK 6–8 and 10–12/US 4–6 and 8–10. The details for the different sizes are separated by a forward slash. If there is no slash, then the details are applicable to both sizes.

Materials and needles

- 500g (17½oz) of 4-ply/sportweight alpaca-blend yarn in dark grey
- 3.5mm (US 4, UK 10) circular knitting needles 80cm (31½in) long and 100cm (39½in) long, or size needed to obtain the correct gauge
- Cable needle
- Blunt-ended needle
- 3 stitch markers

Patterns

Skirt cable (number of stitches at the start divisible by 12): Work following chart 1 (only the odd rounds are shown; on even rounds, work the stitches as they appear), however, work rounds 35–47 four times, work rounds 63–73 four times and rounds 87–95 three times.

Bodice cable pattern: work following chart 2, working in rounds; when you reach the armholes, work backwards and forwards in rows. All rounds and rows are shown.

Seed stitch: *knit 1, purl 1,* repeat from * to *. On the following round or row, purl every knit stitch and knit every purl stitch to create a chequered effect.

Gauge

18 stitches and 24 rows worked in seed stitch using 3.5mm (US 4, UK 10) knitting needles = 10 × 10cm (4 × 4in).

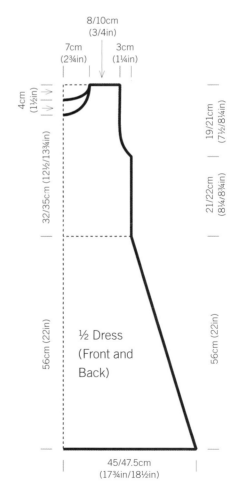

8/10cm
(3/4in)

7cm
(2¾in)

3cm
(1¼in)

4cm
(1½in)

32/35cm (12½/13¾in)

19/21cm
(7½/8¼in)

21/22cm
(8¼/8¾in)

56cm (22in)

56cm (22in)

½ Dress
(Front and
Back)

45/47.5cm
(17¾in/18½in)

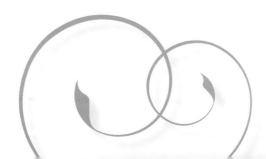

Chart 1 (skirt)

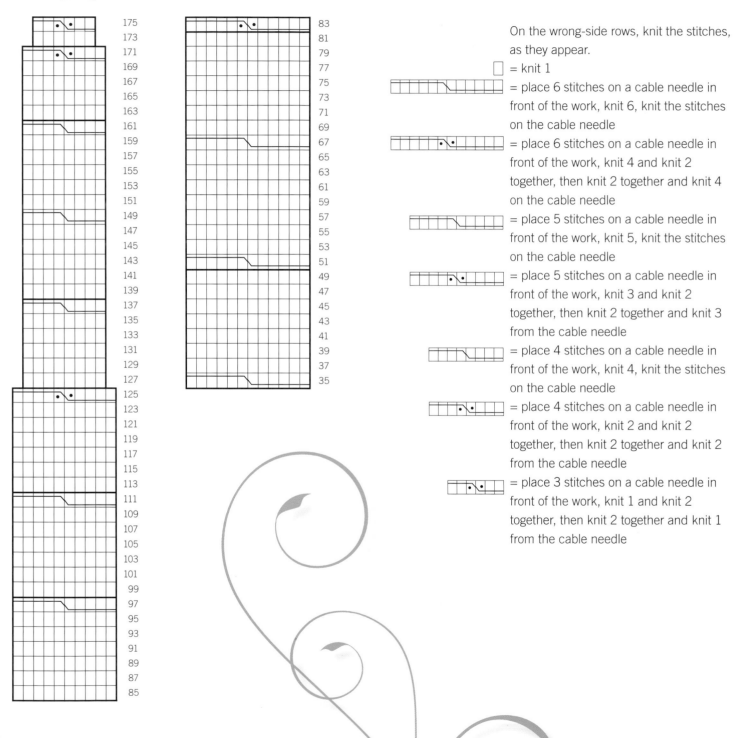

175	83
173	81
171	79
169	77
167	75
165	73
163	71
161	69
159	67
157	65
155	63
153	61
151	59
149	57
147	55
145	53
143	51
141	49
139	47
137	45
135	43
133	41
131	39
129	37
127	35
125	
123	
121	
119	
117	
115	
113	
111	
109	
107	
105	
103	
101	
99	
97	
95	
93	
91	
89	
87	
85	

On the wrong-side rows, knit the stitches, as they appear.

= knit 1

= place 6 stitches on a cable needle in front of the work, knit 6, knit the stitches on the cable needle

= place 6 stitches on a cable needle in front of the work, knit 4 and knit 2 together, then knit 2 together and knit 4 on the cable needle

= place 5 stitches on a cable needle in front of the work, knit 5, knit the stitches on the cable needle

= place 5 stitches on a cable needle in front of the work, knit 3 and knit 2 together, then knit 2 together and knit 3 from the cable needle

= place 4 stitches on a cable needle in front of the work, knit 4, knit the stitches on the cable needle

= place 4 stitches on a cable needle in front of the work, knit 2 and knit 2 together, then knit 2 together and knit 2 from the cable needle

= place 3 stitches on a cable needle in front of the work, knit 1 and knit 2 together, then knit 2 together and knit 1 from the cable needle

Chart 2 (bodice)

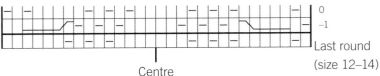

Centre · Last round (size 12–14) · 0 · −1

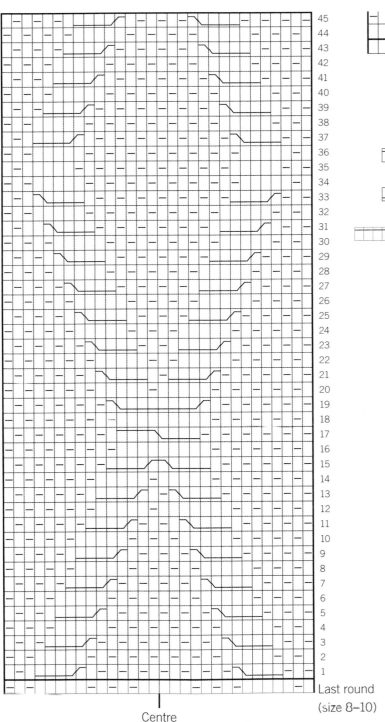

Last round (size 8–10)

Centre

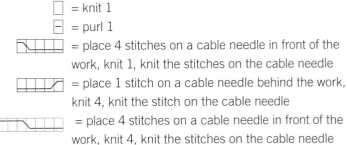

☐ = knit 1

⊟ = purl 1

= place 4 stitches on a cable needle in front of the work, knit 1, knit the stitches on the cable needle

= place 1 stitch on a cable needle behind the work, knit 4, knit the stitch on the cable needle

= place 4 stitches on a cable needle in front of the work, knit 4, knit the stitches on the cable needle

Instructions

The dress is knitted in one piece in rounds as far as the armholes.

Cast on 300/320 stitches and purl 1 row (see the tip). Knit 1 round and then close the work into a round, being careful not to twist the stitches.

Purl 1 round and knit 1 round, then work as follows: *work 12 stitches in stocking stitch, 8 stitches in seed stitch,* repeat from * to * 15/16 times. (The 12 stitches in stocking stitch form the basis for the cable.)

When the piece measures 12cm (4¾in), refer to chart 1 to produce the first cable over the 12 stocking stitches. Continue knitting the 8 stitches in seed stitch in the established pattern. Decrease stitches within the cables as indicated in the chart:

75

by decreasing in the cable pattern, the skirt will taper towards the top.

When the piece measures 56cm (18in), work 3 rounds as the stitches appear, but decreasing either side of each seed-stitch pattern stripe by 1 stitch [150/160 stitches].

Mark the centre front (in the middle of a cable) using a stitch marker. Place another stitch marker 37/39 stitches away from the centre marker on each side: the armholes will start later at these marks.

Slip the stitch markers on every round to keep them on the working round.

Begin knitting in the bodice cable pattern (chart 2). Increase 1 stitch on every other round 8/12 times in seed stitch next to each stitch marker.

When the piece measures 77/78cm (30¼/30¾in), start with the armholes. Do this by dividing the work at the stitch markers and completing the Front and Back pieces separately.

Back

Armhole: at the start of the row, cast off as follows on alternate rows: 4 stitches once, then 2 stitches twice and then 1 stitch 2/4 times.

Neckline: when the piece measures 92/95cm (36¼/37½in), cast off the centre 18 stitches and finish both sides of the Back separately.

On the side of the neckline, cast off as follows on alternate rows: 2 stitches once and then 1 stitch twice.

When the piece measures 96/99cm (37¾/39in), loosely cast off all the stitches.

Front

Armholes: at the start of the row, cast off as follows on alternate rows: 4 stitches once, then 2 stitches once and then 1 stitch twice.

Neckline: when the piece measures 88/91cm (34½/35¾in), cast off the centre 10 stitches and finish both sides of the Front separately.

At the side of the neckline, cast off on alternate rows as follows: 3 stitches once, then 2 stitches twice and then 1 stitch once.

When the piece measures (37¾/39in), loosely cast off all the stitches.

Assembly

Close the shoulder seams.

Carefully stretch out the dress, cover it with damp cloths and leave it to dry.

Cap sleeves: these are knitted on. To do this, pick up 15/21 stitches from the armhole to the right and left of each shoulder seam and work backwards and forwards in rows of seed stitch. Make increases as follows on every other round: 3 stitches twice and then 2 stitches twice.

After 2cm (¾in) in seed stitch, work in rounds over the whole armhole, knit 1 round, purl 1 round, knit 1 round and purl 1 round. On the following round, loosely cast off all the stitches knitwise. Work the second sleeve in the same way.

Neckline trim: pick up 108/118 stitches from the neckline on the right side of the work and knit 1 round, purl 1 round, knit 1 round, purl 1 round. On the following round, loosely cast off all the stitches, knitwise.

Darn in all the yarn ends.

Tip

As so many stitches have to be cast on for this dress, we recommend that you work two rows and then close the work into a round. This way, it is easier to see whether the stitches on the needle have twisted. This also avoids any little knots appearing on the outside of the work after casting on in the normal way.

Tip

Cables involving more than 6 stitches can be made flatter by working in the following way: make a yarn over in the round in front of the cabling between each of the stitches that are placed behind the work when cabling. Slip these yarn overs when cabling. This will make the stitches larger and the cable lies flatter.

First published in Great Britain 2012 by Search Press Limited,
Wellwood, North Farm Road, Tunbridge Wells, Kent TN2 3DR

Original German edition published as *Märchenhaft Stricken*

Copyright © 2010 Christophorus Verlag GmbH & Co. KG, Freiburg
Alle Rechte vorbehalten

English translation by Cicero Translations

English edition typeset by GreenGate Publishing Services

ISBN: 978-1-84448-743-1

Idea, designs and production: Katharina Ritter
Photography: Antonio Pruthete, A3gency
Styling: Helen Anderson
Technical drawings: Johanna Heiß

Manufacturers' details
ggh Garn Großhandel Hamburg GmbH, Pinneberg, Germany, www.ggh-garn.de

Filatura di Crosa, over Lanartus Garnimport GmbH, Inzlingen, Germany, www.lanartus.net

Lang Yarns, Reithe (CH), Switzerland, www.longyarns.ch

Lana Grossa, Gaimersheim, Germany,
www.lanagrossa.de

Coats GmbH, Salach, Germany, www.coatsgmbh.de

The author would like to thank the yarn manufacturers for their generous support.